THE
TRANSFORMATIONAL
ENTREPRENEUR

Engaging The Mind, Heart, And Spirit
For Breakthrough Business Success

Terry Murray

Performance Transformation, LLC

www.performtransform.com

ISBN: 978-0-615-45462-7

To my wife, Sarah.

CONTENTS

Introduction

If you've been dreaming of starting your own business, you're not alone. According to the Small Business Administration, Office of Advocacy, there are an estimated 12.6 million "nascent entrepreneurs" in the United States.[1] In their 2008 report, "The Small Business Economy, A Report To The President", the Small Business Administration defines a nascent entrepreneur as someone that is seriously contemplating starting a business. This incubation period for nascent entrepreneurs will typically last five years, at which time a third will have launched a business, a third will have disengaged from the pursuit, and a third will continue to think about it. This isn't a period of idle daydreaming. The report goes on to identify the average nascent entrepreneur will invest 1,471 hours (the equivalent of nine months of 40 hour work weeks) and $10,734 of their own money during this pre-launch period. Cumulatively, a total of $60 billion in informal, financial contributions are expended every year by individuals that,

---

[1] "The Small Business Economy, A Report To The President", SBA, Office of Advocacy, 2008.

for the most part, will not personally benefit from these investments. That's truly putting your money where your mouth is!

Entrepreneurs are the lifeblood of the U.S. economy and continue to kindle the flames of the American Dream. Small businesses employ half of all private sector employees, produce half of the country's non-farm Gross Domestic Product, and create roughly 75% of new private sector jobs.[2] Perhaps more importantly, small firms produce 50% of new innovations[3] and are a major source of significant market changes.[4] Entrepreneurs built the United States, and it is the entrepreneurial spirit that is pulling our nation out of the Great Recession.

Entrepreneurs move us all forward, yet they face tremendous headwinds in the pursuit of their dreams. Government regulations disproportionately burden small businesses as compared to large corporations and their

---

[2] "The INTUIT Future of Small Business Series", Institute for the Future, 2007.

[3] Audretsch, David B. (1995). "Innovation and Industry Evolution." Cambridge, MA: MIT Press.

[4] Baumol, William J. (2005). "Small Firms: Why Market-Driven Innovation Can't Get Along Without Them." SBA, U.S. Government Printing Office, Washington, D.C.

wealth of resources. Large corporate concerns spend vast amounts of money lobbying our state and federal governments, entrenching their interests, often at the expense of individuals and small businesses. Often, the mere size of corporations can dominate entire market segments, creating barriers to entry for innovative, nimble competitors capable of shifting entire value propositions. Yet the entrepreneurial spirit continues to thrive.

I should probably tell you a little about myself. I shipped off to the Navy when I was seventeen years old and served aboard an aircraft carrier as a Naval Intelligence Specialist. This was where my foundation was forged. Naval Intelligence taught me a set of skills that still serve me today. They introduced me to strategic planning, albeit military strategic planning, but strategic planning nonetheless. They taught me how to comb through myriad amounts of data, discern what was of strategic importance, convert data into targeting information, create step-by-step strike plans, and instilled my ability to communicate these plans on an executive level. The Navy also imparted a life-and-death sense of responsibility for my work as the lives of highly trained pilots and my shipmates depended on my accuracy and attention to detail. Before I was nineteen years old, like so many of our service personnel today, I was accountable for other people's lives. This sense of responsibility and accountability towards the people that depend on my work has never left me. It has proven to be a key accelerant and differentiator in my career.

I went on to study business administration in college and found myself, upon graduation, working as a sales representative in the rapidly emerging biotechnology industry in Cambridge, Massachusetts. After six years in field sales, carrying a bag as we used to say, I began my managerial career, quickly matriculating up the chain of command in a variety of large corporations. By the time I was 36 years old I was Vice President of Sales and Marketing for Europe, the Middle East, and Africa for a billion dollar medical device company. I had complete profit and loss responsibility (true accountability) and hundreds of people (very real responsibility) working for me.

Eventually tiring of the politics of corporate life, I headed into the start-up world in my late thirties. After helping two start-up companies get off the ground I went to work as a consultant and Executive Strategist in the emerging business and start-up community. Over the last decade, I've had the privilege to conduct strategic assessments for dozens of companies, create strategic launch plans, help start-ups obtain investment capital, and guide them to secure initial sales traction in their markets. I found myself being paid to continue learning about the dynamics of bringing new businesses to market while leveraging the real-world education I had received in the resource-rich world of Corporate America.

This period of time coincided with what could best be described as my own spiritual awakening. Through study and reflection, I began to identify patterns in business that previously appeared unexplainable to me. A new clarity began to emerge, and with it a vision of how human beings think, feel, and function within businesses. With this came a sense of purpose and a desire to be of greater service to the community. My community, for the past decade, has been one populated by entrepreneurs.

Three years ago, I began searching for books that reflected the importance of engaging the mind, heart, and spirit of human beings in business. Books that explored leadership from an enlightened perspective. The books I found on the subject tended towards relatively vague, etherial platitudes, or collections of success anecdotes about spiritually progressive business people, but little in the way of the actual processes and action items that could accelerate entrepreneurial success. The mission-critical factors of the professional community in which I live, work, and attempt to serve. Thus, the seeds of this book were sown. This book is an attempt to share the real-world processes of grounded, start-up business practice that actually work examined from the perspective of a growing spiritual awareness. Fore it is through spiritual awareness that businesses can truly engage the entire human continuum of its workforce; the creativity, the passion, and the dedication start-ups desperately need to secure traction against the headwinds they all face.

I've been blessed to work both sides of the street, developing the skills and perspective that could have only emerged from walking my rather unusual path. One key lesson I've learned along the way is it is critically important to identify what not to do and where not to go in business as quickly as possible. In sales, we call it "getting to no" quickly. Great sales people don't mind being told no; they do mind being told maybe and wasting their valuable time in pursuit of opportunities that will never bear fruit. This concept is even more important for entrepreneurs.

Why do I bring this up? Digging deeper into the Small Business Administration's report reveals several important issues within the nascent entrepreneur community. First, six in ten nascent entrepreneurs report that this is their first start-up. Another critical lesson I've come to appreciate is we don't know what we don't know. If this is your first rodeo, it is difficult to know where to even begin. In addition, when we consider that more than half of all entrepreneurs have less than six years of managerial experience, very few have enjoyed the privilege of being intimately involved in the strategic planning process.

This is perhaps why only 48% of nascent entrepreneurs have initiated a business plan (the government report doesn't reveal how many have actually completed the planning process). Yet, at the same time, 81% of them are investing their own money and a significant amount of their time and energy. To quote the SBA report, "It is reasonable to expect the startup process to require the equivalent of one year of full-time work and tens of thousands of dollars." By following the step-by-step planning process I've laid out in this book, nascent entrepreneurs can quickly and affordably discern the viability of their idea and hopefully go on to secure market traction before breaking their own bank.

I'd like to quote a few more insightful findings from the SBA report:

"The major factors affecting success in completing the startup process with a new business are related to what is actually done to implement a new firm and the work experience of the individual."

"What entrepreneurs do is much more important than who they are."

"So what is the bottom line for aspiring entrepreneurs? Know what you are doing and do it."

And...

"The most effective way to increase the probability of success is to provide training and managerial assistance to active nascent entrepreneurs. Substantive training and education creates a fuller understanding of future customers, markets, and industry practices - information that can lead to the identification of opportunities. Having the skills and information needed to implement a new firm will facilitate developing new ventures that reflect emerging business opportunities."

That is what this book is about. Providing a proven methodology that I've used for more than two decades of business success. This book isn't about meditating your way to success or how the power of positive thinking will automatically draw success into your fold. Yes, those things may be important, but it is the actions you take combined with your positive intention and mindfulness that will be the ultimate determining factor in your success.

And with that, I sincerely wish all of you the best of luck in the pursuit of your dreams!

The Transformational Entrepreneur

Chapter One ~
A New Approach to Business As Usual
"Hands to Work, Hearts to God." Old Shaker Saying

I recently watched documentarian Ken Burns' 1985 film, "The Shakers". It had been many years since I had first seen it. It is a familiar film on a familiar subject. Mr. Burns' production company, Florentine Films, operates in the tiny, Yankee hamlet of Walpole, NH, where my father grew up and I spent many a languid, summer afternoon as a boy. Swimming with my cousins, riding their horses, picking sweet corn fresh from the field ten minutes before it was to find the boiling pot, day dreaming under ancient maples along the Connecticut River on still August days. The pace of that little town is reflected in Mr. Burns' films; he always gives the story the time it seems to want, the time it seems to need, to unfold in gentle rhythms before us.

My father was an antiques dealer, and so, on occasion, a piece of Shaker furniture would find its way into our shop. It was a living shop, meaning we lived with the continuously turning inventory populating the various rooms of the old colonial in which we dwelled. Every

1

drawer of the candle stands (we'd call them end tables today), every lid of the blanket boxes, had a price tag adhered to the interior. I remember what a time of joy it was when a Shaker piece, made by the hands of a gifted craftsperson a generation or two before the Civil War, would find its way into our lives, if only for a few days or weeks. There was a simple elegance of design, purposeful and sturdy, that immediately told of its providence. An elegance that differentiated it from the many other fine Hepplewhite and Sheraton pieces from the same era.

The Shakers were a community of Christians that chose to live their lives in communal celibacy, living each day in worship to God. They were the first egalitarian Christian society in the New World, each community being led by two men and two women (the Elders and Eldresses).

They had two communities in New Hampshire, one in Enfield and another in Canterbury, just a few miles north of our capital, Concord (which of course, we pronounced, "Cawncud", drawing out the first syllable until almost breathless, and nearly swallowing the second), which I was fortunate enough to visit as a young man while the two surviving Eldresses were still alive. They were an industrious and imaginative people, inventing the first circular saw, improving the simple broom from round to flat (not a minor improvement if you've ever swept a room with a round broom), and perfecting the mail order seed business, among many others. And they designed and built some of the finest furniture the world has ever seen. Each Shaker rotated through the various jobs in the community on a monthly basis, learning every trade and craft, ensuring there was no weak link in the function of their lives and industry.

The Shakers' authentic, spiritual nature resonates, for over two centuries now, in every surviving artifact they produced. Much like the Amish, the Quakers, and the Mennonites, they did not believe in adornment (to the Amish, even buttons are seen as "proud" and hooks are traditionally used to fasten their clothing). Their designs are simple, functional, and clean, yet reflect a sophisticated and quiet elegance that seems lost in our time of obsessive Tweeting, texting, and superfluous distractions. They somehow subjugated their ego and expressed their love of God, and their love of humankind, in every task they performed. For the Shakers, work was a form of worship. No task was menial, no hierarchy of importance existed in work. If it needed to be done it was to be done towards the goal of perfection in honor of their faith. Every community could have proudly displayed a sign at the entrance of their workshops, "Consultants Need Not Apply".

The generosity of their spirit and fruits of their labor were noteworthy. Seeing the local indigents stealing from their fields, they would plant extra crops for them to take, never saying a word. When autumn would blow in with its biting, damp wind, the "Winter Shakers" would arrive, profess their desire to convert, and promptly leave with the warming sun of the spring. The Shakers did not mind. They felt that if it was meant to be, the Spirit would show itself in time in these folks. As I sit and write this I am admiring one of my late father's Enfield ladderback chairs, crafted by a Shaker some 170 years ago. It is as sturdy and beautiful as the day the varnish dried. A chair that has been sat in by more than five generations and that is still perfectly functional today. This simple yet amazing chair that was perfectly constructed without the benefit of Total Quality Systems, Six Sigma, or Value-Add Committees.

I reflect on the culture, philosophy, and spirit of the people who produced such industry and elegance; who produced this chair. It seems as out of place in our current culture and business climate as if it had emerged from another planet, yet it also represents hope to me. Hope that we, as human beings, can still find the courage to suspend our egos, seek authenticity in our lives, and view our work as a form of spiritual practice.

A variety of forces conspired to eventually winnow away at the Shaker communities. Laws were passed forbidding them to take in orphans (young people were free to leave the communities upon adulthood or choose to stay) and the Industrial Revolution brought in mass production that eroded prices and disrupted their markets for woven goods, furniture, and medicines. And of course, celibacy can be a bit of a self-limiting constraint to generational growth.

Ten years into the new millennium the limitations of the economic and social forces that marked the shift from our agrarian and cottage industry past have become painfully apparent. The command-and-control, hierarchical structures and business cultures that grew out of the Industrial Revolution that swept away a simpler time have also grown tired and corrupt. During the Industrial Revolution and well into the twentieth century, value was created through the exploitation of cheap, abundant raw materials combined with specialized, relatively low skilled labor, and capital. Throughout the latter part of the nineteenth century, and most of the twentieth century, everyday goods, from textiles to furniture, and from appliances to automobiles, were manufactured in the United States to be consumed by the United States. Economies of scale and vertical integration were key drivers of efficient commerce. Command-and-control, central planning, and rigid hierarchies emerged to drive these efficiencies. While all of this ushered in an era of unprecedented wealth it also had its drawbacks. Work as spiritual practice is difficult to sustain while toiling away on an assembly line.

The source of today's value creation has, however, shifted from exploiting resources to embracing knowledge workers capable of creating commercially viable intellectual property. One might expect that such a fundamental shift in the source of business value would drive a corresponding shift in management and leadership philosophy. It seems that one should have naturally followed the other, yet most companies still hold fast to an antiquated approach to management. The application of information technology has bridged the emerging gap between value source and managerial process since the

1980's, but the productivity benefits of this approach are reaching the point of diminishing returns.

So where do we look to create a new paradigm of leadership and managerial process that optimizes the contemporary source of business value? If we look back to the leaders of the industrial revolution and early twentieth century we see remarkable innovation and creativity applied to the opportunities and constraints of the day. People like Henry Ford and Alfred Sloan literally invented new ways of organizing, managing, and applying the emerging technology of their time. The imperative source of value creation today (continuously evolving intellectual property) is as vital to us as the assembly line and newly created corporate management structure was to them. Shouldn't we take an equally innovative approach to optimizing this new source of value today as our predecessors did nearly a century ago?

The intention of this book is to introduce a new perspective on leadership, managerial process, and business culture that cultivates the source of value creation in the twenty-first century; human beings. The ideas put forth on the following pages may seem as revolutionary as the ideas that took root one hundred years ago, but the time for change is long overdue. Simply put, there has to be a better way of fully engaging and leveraging the talents of human beings working in businesses today. The competitive advantages that machinery, automation, and information technology may have once delivered are no longer the differentiators in the global knowledge economy. It is people that make the difference and this requires a new, conscious approach to how we perceive ourselves as business leaders and how we view, inspire, and care for those that work around us.

Traditional management principles are rooted in neo-classical economic theory which views people as "rational actors" who will optimize utility in their economic behaviors. Any deviations are leveled through the "invisible hand" of aggregate market forces. The emerging discipline of Applied Behavioral Economics (an integration of psychology and economics) reveals the underlying fallacy of these precepts. Leading behavioral economists concur that economic decision making is actually 70% emotionally driven and only 30% rationally driven. Human beings are emotional creatures. Emotions emerged in mammals as part of our primary survival mechanisms. Our emotions inform us as to the dangers and opportunities in our environment. They are as intrinsic to us as our senses of sight, touch, taste, smell, and hearing, yet contemporary management practices attempt to disengage us from our natural state of being, diminishing emotions as a messy bi-product that needs to be compartmentalized and best left at home.

When we are disengaged from our authentic nature is it any wonder why we become disengaged from those around us, our work, and our employers? This is a logical result of leading people from a perspective set in false premises. Remember the tragic episode involving the tiger and Siegfried and Roy, when the tiger suddenly attacked Roy Horn during their Las Vegas act? People were shocked that the tiger suddenly went "crazy". Comedian Chris Rock made an insightful observation of the incident when he said the tiger didn't go crazy, the tiger went tiger. A master predator was placed in the most unnatural circumstances a tiger could find itself. We're doing the same thing with human beings, placing them in unnatural circumstances, setting unprecedented behavioral expectations upon them, and expecting them to act against their nature, and then wondering why we are experiencing an employee engagement crisis.

When we disrupt a human being's ability to be whole, to disengage a person from what I call our human continuum, we also disengage them from the source of their creativity and natural brilliance...their spirit. The spark of innovation, initiative, and inspiration that is our natural gift from the mysterious Divine. This crowning aspect of our human continuum, our spiritual nature, where Creator endows creativity, is the very essence of what is needed for businesses to compete in our new economy. It is time once again to approach our work as a form of spiritual practice.

Intellectual property is the raw material of the new century. Whether we are discussing biotechnology, telecommunications, nanotechnology, software, or professional services, intellectual property is the kernel of value creation. It emerges from human creative consciousness, and evolves towards the creation of commercial products and services through the work of highly skilled teams. Success today requires cooperative teams of knowledge workers that have an entirely different set of expectations from our predecessors living in the Industrial Age. Creativity comes from the heart as much as it does from the head. It turns out how people *feel* about their work is as important, if not more important, than what they *think* about their work.

If Henry Ford's assembly lines weren't working at full capacity and were prone to breaking down he would have addressed them immediately. He would have fixed the problem. Yet when we examine the human factor in businesses today we tend to see an unaddressed fracture in the source of modern value creation; worker engagement.

I think it is safe to say we have all experienced or witnessed friends or family members that are disengaged and generally apathetic about their work situation. Research into worker engagement supports this observation. A recent, highly regarded national polling corporation conducted a study that indicated more than 70% of employees are not engaged or are actively disengaged (17% are actively working at cross purpose with their employers) from their work and organization. The study identifies the fact that only one out of every four employees is actively engaged with their work, meaning the employee works with passion and is highly connected to their organization. They are the ones that drive innovation and continuously move their company forward. Employees that are not engaged are *sleepwalking* through work and those that are actively disengaged actually work to undermine their fellow associates on a regular basis. Still another recent study indicates that companies that enjoy employee engagement levels that are above the average in their business sector enjoy 17% higher operating margins! A quick internet search on "worker engagement" will reveal these studies and dozens more supporting this viewpoint.

Analysis of the employee engagement crises conducted by my firm, Performance Transformation, LLC reveals an even more startling result. Even if we give the sleep-walking employees the benefit of the doubt, that they're contributing value half of the time, a typical company can expect a zero return on investment on approximately 57% of their payroll! Would Henry Ford have accepted a 57% scrap rate on raw materials? I highly doubt it, but that's exactly what is happening when we realize human capital is the raw material in today's economy. Unfortunately, most companies appear to be at a loss in their ability to embrace this data and act accordingly to fix what is broken in their organizations.

This engagement crisis is exacerbated by the fact that our world is in transition. Command-and-Control, hierarchical businesses struggle with adapting to even minor changes. When confronted with economic challenges they tend to do what they know and are comfortable doing. They acquire competitors and consolidate overhead (i.e. layoffs). They spin off underperforming business to fend for themselves and not depress their stock price. They continuously migrate their manufacturing to the lowest cost environment. They seek value through cutting rather than creating. Traditional companies engage in a nearly schizophrenic cycle of hiring and firing, of expansion and contraction. There is an inherent unsustainability to this approach due to the negative effects it has on human beings, but somehow this is rarely taken into account in the board room.

As a result of this cyclical, shortsighted behavior, the United States is now a debtor nation with precarious, endemic trade deficits compounded by an eroding manufacturing base. The only edge the U.S. maintains in the global economy is creativity, and even this is beginning to diffuse around the world. Simultaneously, the East is on the rise. India and China are rapidly investing in educating knowledge workers, positioning themselves to strategically catapult beyond their current position as the low-cost providers of manufacturing and support labor for the West. Their coming emergence will be accompanied by their cultural norms and perspectives of what it is to be a human being.

We are also experiencing a generational shift. Young workers, the so-called Generation Y, have a different set of expectations for career and life. They seek a level of fulfillment and balance the now retiring Baby Boomers were willing to forgo in exchange for economic stability. Having come to adulthood over the past two decades they have witnessed the legions of workers that gave their lives to a single company only to be displaced at the next economic downturn. Younger workers, and especially knowledge workers, are quite willing to take their talents to another employer. They don't have the expectation of working for a single company for thirty years. They are very comfortable hop-scotching from one three year engagement to the next as long as it serves their career path and expectations of fulfillment.

The combination of these factors is setting the stage for unprecedented change. We are simultaneously experiencing a seminal change in the source of value creation, a generational shift in worker expectations, the accelerating retirement of highly experienced Baby Boomers, and a geopolitical shift in the economic influence of the East. The cumulative influences of these factors share a common undercurrent. The global knowledge workers of today, the emerging leaders of the future, and the business leaders of the East do not see the world in the same way as the business leaders we typically find at the helm of U.S. business today. The human element has never been more influential in the success or failure of companies. The perceptions and expectations of this human element are fundamentally different than that of the people that framed the success of the past. This is the source of the disconnection, and the clinging of outmoded leadership philosophy and business methods perpetuates and exacerbates associate disengagement.

To paraphrase Albert Einstein, "Problems cannot be solved by the same level of consciousness that created them". Yet, in many ways, this is what we are seeing in contemporary business. The organizational structure, controlling management processes, and leadership attitudes that emerged out of the Industrial Age, the very level of consciousness that created the disconnect, is struggling to acknowledge and address the situation. A transformation needs to occur that enables businesses to evolve and thrive in this new world.

Lasting transformation emerges from an inner shift in perspective; the catalytic power that comes through the igniting of consciousness. Carl Jung, the founder of analytical psychiatry, perhaps said it best, "Your vision will become clear only when you look into your heart...Who looks outside dreams. Who looks inside, awakens." In order for a new business paradigm to emerge that addresses the remarkable opportunities of this new world, leadership must look into their hearts. It is in the heart that we find passion; the passion to inspire, to innovate, and to fully engage the people that constitute organizations and are the source of creativity.

The path of self reflection, of continuously discovering the perennial wisdom that lies within us all, is not something commonly taught in Western business schools. As Westerners, we tend to look exclusively outward for answers; to science and technology to address the shortcomings of process and the need for improvement.

For several millennia, our Eastern counterparts have taken a different approach, of looking inward for the answers to life's greatest questions and challenges. While the traditional philosophies of the East may seem quite foreign to contemporary Western thinking, it is interesting to contemplate the evolution of Quantum Physics over the past eighty years. This mathematical and theoretical exploration of our perceptions of physical form have lifted a veil, revealing a higher awareness that in many ways parallels the ancient Eastern spiritual perspective of the formless. Can it be a coincidence that the giants of twentieth century physics, Einstein, Schroedinger, Heisenberg, De Broglie, Jeans, Planck, Pauli, and Eddington all, in some form and degree, became mystics during their lives?[5]

By taking a more inclusive view of human beings, of our hearts and spirits as well as our intellect and physical nature, business leaders can begin to formulate new paradigms. New approaches that will empower not simply a continuous, competitive advantage but the flourishing, preferential benefits that move us beyond surviving to the wondrous possibility of thriving!

---

[5] Ken Wilber's book, "Quantum Questions, Mystical Writings of the World's Greatest Physicists." Shambhalla, Boston, 2001 provides an excellent collection of the mystical perspectives these men came to embraced during their lifetimes.

This shift in perspective is already starting to take root. Western business leaders and thinkers are slowly beginning to embrace the need for an evolutionary approach to management and leadership. In the Business Spirit Journal Online, author and consultant Jeff Hutner reported on the findings presented by Michael Rennie, then a partner with McKinsey & Company, and Gita Bellin, at the International Conference on Business and Consciousness held in Puerto Vallarta, Mexico in 1998. Mr. Rennie and Ms. Bellin developed a three day workshop to help McKinsey clients develop a more spiritual approach to their work environment, helping them to migrate from their head to their heart. The results? One client that was experiencing a 35% turnover rate experienced a decline of 65% in four months. Several other clients experienced a 400% increase in productivity.[6]

Mr. Rennie, who went on to direct McKinsey & Company's Global Mindsets and Capabilities Practice, was quoted in an article appearing in 2005 in Training and Coaching Today:

---

[6] http://www.bizspirit.com/bsj/archive/articles/hutner1.html, Jeff Hutner, Business Spirit Journal Online, Issue #34.

"If you look at what brings energy into a team, increasingly it's about the idea that we are people, not machines. You do that through a combination of values and high purpose - spiritual intelligence, for lack of a better term - coupled with the right sort of interactions and learning." He added, "People are two to five times more productive in that kind of environment. That is what's required in companies today - to be collaborative to succeed. The big thing to come out of this is for leaders to realize that meaning is the big motivating driver."[7]

From my own personal experience of more than twenty years working with global life science and medical device companies I can honestly say I have never seen a business endeavor fail due to the technology. Success or failure consistently lies at the feet of management. Having spent the last ten years working with start-up companies, the greatest challenge I have witnessed investors struggling with is not in finding ample technologies worthy of investment, but in finding inspirational leadership capable of igniting and leveraging the power of positive intention.

---

[7] http://www.personneltoday.com/articles/2005/07/13/30761/meaningful-management.html, Margaret Kubicek, Training and Coaching Today, July 13, 2005.

The application of these technologies is often remarkably promising to the human condition, offering effective treatments to end suffering, lower health care expenditures, and improve overall accessibility of medical care to a broader proportion of the population. In other words, these technologies offer promise and positive meaning to the venture and the world. Yet, even with this meaningful, humanistic purpose, leadership often stumbles along the road to market. Traditional business structure, culture, and process became the choke point of innovation rather than its catalyst.

The challenge today's business leaders face is how to migrate to a new management paradigm that cultivates creativity and efficiently commercializes intellectual property without introducing untenable risk to the enterprise. This is no small task in that this is terra incognito to many executives. There is a pathway, however, that enables businesses to transform their culture and unleash their human capital, delivering breakthrough performance while mitigating risk. This is the journey we are undertaking together. We will explore a step-by-step, practical methodology that will bring this new approach to business into being.

~ The Need for Conscious Leadership

The first step begins with a shift in perspective, a self-reflective awakening of consciousness in leadership. A new way of doing cannot emerge without first discovering a new way of being. When we speak of conscious leadership we are speaking of a very simple premise. It is leadership that is self-aware and fully present in the moment. A perspective that is consciously aware of what is simultaneously "with-in" and "with-out" at any given moment. Leadership that is not just doing in the present moment, but leadership that is being in the present moment as well. Leadership that is truly authentic in and of its self.

Let's step back for a moment and reflect on the dysfunctional business cultures we have all been a part of at one time or another during our careers. Chances are, they have been hierarchical, command and control structures that emphasize one-dimensional performance; of "hitting the number". The organization is rife with strife, people competing against one another in an attempt to make it up the next rung of the ladder. Passive aggressive behavior is rampant, and strangely enough, often rewarded. The cultural landscape is likely populated by aggressive, "Type-A" personalities that are willing to do most anything to gratify themselves and deliver their version of personal success. What some colleagues and I used to refer to as Corporate Darwinism. But what was it that enabled this dysfunction to overtake the culture of the organization? I'm not implying senior management was malicious in their intent, but that they were not fully aware of the power of the culture they had unconsciously unleashed upon the organization. As long as the number was met, everything else, short of overtly unethical behavior and breaking the law, was pretty much tolerated.

The organizational culture was trapped in an endless cycle of human insecurity and fear. Associates, from the leadership on down throughout the hierarchy, were driven by a fear of not hitting the number next month, next quarter, next year. Extraordinary energy was expended by continuous positioning and posturing in order to hide perceived weaknesses or past failures from one another. The entire organization was being motivated by negative energy rooted in perceptions of the past (regret) and projections into the future (fear). Associates spent little, if any, time in the present and the vibration of anxiety was prevalent every single day. Any of us that have worked in a large corporation can probably relate to this observation. I can remember a five year stretch of time in my life when I never enjoyed a good night's sleep on a Sunday, my mind racing with thoughts of the coming day, the coming week, the coming quarter.

Conscious leadership can break this cycle of wasted energy and effort, but it must start with its self. In doing so, a new and powerful awareness will emerge and this new awareness, this new consciousness, can sow the seeds of a creative, cooperative business culture that is capable of transforming the entire company without introducing disruptive risk to the organization.

We can begin this transformation by contemplating a few, simple ideas that can help us shift our perceptions of our selves as well as those working and living around us. First put forth in his 1923 book, "The Prophet", Kahlil Gibran states that we are not human beings placed upon this earth to have a spiritual experience, but spiritual beings here to have a human experience. Many contemporary spiritual thinkers express a very similar understanding of the human condition. There is more to us than a job description and viewing humans in this way limits our natural, creative capabilities. We also need to consider that the moments of transformational inspiration come during the quiet moments, from our deep, inner consciousness. Albert Einstein often spoke that his insights and moments of breakthrough clarity did not come while toiling over reams of equations, but at the most innocuous times; when he was away from his work enjoying a simple moment. A moment of stillness that brings us closer to our authentic selves.

Our consciousness is our essence. It lies quietly below our learned behavior and the constant noise of this hectic world and of our mental state (the continuous conversation we have with ourselves in our head). By becoming aware of this we can begin to experience a shift in our traditional, learned perspectives of what it is to lead and manage a business.

Conscious leadership can create an environment, an atmosphere, a thriving culture that draws people into the present moment. It is capable of alleviating anxieties by building a sense of trust, genuine empathy, and engaged commitment that will help quiet the mind and cultivate a creative, transformational consciousness within the organization. It is more than just intent; it is an evolutionary process that integrates leadership with mindful strategic planning, execution, and talent management.

Through the application of this process, new paradigms will emerge. A new clarity will rapidly come into focus throughout the entire organization. One capable of creating and delivering the differentiating value all companies seek but rarely enjoy.

~ Key Concepts

- The source of business value has evolved from exploiting raw materials, labor, and capital to the cultivation of human creativity. Human beings are the differentiating value in contemporary business.

- The approach of leadership and the business paradigms that were developed during the Industrial Age are failing to fully cultivate human creativity. The majority of people are disengaged from their work and organizations.

- Humans are not one-dimensional beings. In order to truly inspire human beings, leadership must engage their minds, hearts, and spirits.

- A new consciousness needs to emerge in business leadership in order to create transformational business performance.

Chapter Two ~
Igniting Transformational Performance

"If you have built castles in the air, your work need not be lost; that is where they should be. Now put the foundations under them." Henry David Thoreau

Creating transformational performance is like igniting a fire; it requires three fundamental elements. A fire requires a source of heat, fuel, and oxygen in order to burn. Transformational performance requires authentic, conscious leadership (the heat), a visionary strategic plan (the fuel), and a creative culture that fully engages the entire workforce (the oxygen).

While transformational performance cannot occur without all three elements, the quality of leadership will greatly enhance or diminish both the ascendance and long-term success of a business. The intensity of its energy and the clarity of its intention can emulate that of a paper match or an acetylene torch.

The quality of the strategic plan will influence sustainability and growth; it can take the form of seasoned hardwood or half-rotted pulp. The final element, culture,

27

can fan or extinguish the brightest leadership and the most thoughtful strategies. Like oxygen, we cannot literally see culture, yet it is the air we all breathe.

~ Authentic Leadership

Leading a business requires a strong and unflinching sense of responsibility for the associates who depend upon your wisdom, integrity, and stewardship. Their livelihoods, dreams, and aspirations are invested in your guidance. This is a sacred trust. Associates trust that you will do your best to ensure the health and vitality of the business. The stronger their level of trust in your leadership, the more willing they will be to fully invest their time, energy, and enthusiasm in the success of the endeavor. The level of authenticity a leader expresses in their daily interactions with people and in how they address challenging situations will have an enormous impact on execution.

Authenticity may sound like an unusual word to describe leadership, but its meaning reflects several key characteristics that are critical to successfully leading human beings. There are three primary definitions of authenticity in the dictionary; the quality of being authentic, trustworthy or genuine, and the displaying of undisputed credibility.

The quality of being authentic begins with being true to one's self. This quality emerges through self reflection and inner exploration and infers an active awareness of one's consciousness. The complete spectrum of who we are physically, intellectually, emotionally, and spiritually. This includes being in touch with, and trusting in, one's own intuition. We'll explore the role of intuition further in Chapter Four.

At times, being true to one's self isn't easy. It can test our moral courage. In the late 1990's while serving as the vice president of sales and marketing for a highly acquisitive life science company I experienced this conflict. I found myself confronted with having to decide whether I would lead with authenticity or "go along to get along".

Shortly after our company purchased a small manufacturing concern we found ourselves with two mid-level executives with overlapping responsibilities for managing our European sales business. One was from our organization and one arrived with the acquired company. The president of our company had sidestepped a decision on realigning responsibilities for two months. The new executive was very political and focused much of his efforts and energy to develop a social relationship with the president, inviting him to play golf and entertaining him at his home. After more than a year of diligent work on the part of our director to build our business in Europe the ambiguity began wearing on his emotions and productivity.

The situation left me uneasy at what I felt was inherently unfair. At the very least, our director deserved a word of clarification on the issue. Finally, on a Friday afternoon preceding our director leaving on a scheduled trip to meet with our European partners (who would be looking for direction and clarification as well) I felt compelled to address the situation with the president. My inquiry infuriated the president who proceeded to lash out verbally. I took some lumps and expended significant political capital, but my authentic concern for my direct report resonated throughout the sales and marketing organization, building trust and resulting in measurably marked improvements in sales performance.

As the years progressed, I began to realize my sensibilities of leadership didn't correlate with what I was consistently experiencing in Corporate America. While my performance was frequently lauded by my superiors, I would eventually find myself at odds with the status quo. Somehow, my presence made my fellow executives uncomfortable. Our intentions didn't match. I eventually came to the realization I didn't belong in this environment and made the decision to strike out on my own and start a business focusing on coaching entrepreneurs on leadership, strategy, and business process. In discovering and following my authentic self I now work from a position of service that has created the greatest joy and satisfaction I have ever experienced in my life!

The second definition of authenticity is "trustworthy or genuine". Trust is an energy that flows in a circular orbit. It cannot move in one direction without returning to whence it came. Some people allow themselves to trust more readily than others, but once trust has been broached it is often nearly impossible to mend.

Cultivating a trustworthy environment dispels people's fears and calms insecurities. It enables people to function in the moment without worrying about the repercussions of making an honest mistake. The legendary salesman and early leader of IBM, Thomas J. Watson, was once quoted as saying, "Recently, I was asked if I was going to fire an employee who made a mistake that cost the company

$600,000. No, I replied, I just spent $600,000 training him. Why would I want somebody to hire his experience?"

Sometimes we learn more from our mistakes and allowing for the occasional mistake without the anticipation or fear of punishment builds trust. Trusting associates empowers people to work from their heart which draws upon the energy of positive intention. It opens the door to passionate engagement and reveals the *hidden workforce* lying quietly just beneath the surface in many businesses. Creating an environment that encourages mature, thoughtful risk-taking delivers returns that far exceed any potential losses.

In the context of our discussion, the definition of "genuine" refers to being from the original stock or lineage, of being a genuine human being. This implies we see each other as universally and energetically connected as a single entity of creation. In doing so, we are able to express empathy for one another as easily and openly as we are able to care about our selves. The resonant power of empathy consistently expressed by leadership cannot be overestimated. It conveys genuine concern and respect for an associate's well-being. In doing so, it lowers barriers and engages the heart as well as the mind. It is something we all can relate to. Ask yourself, how much more are you willing to do for someone that genuinely cares about you?

Several years ago I was engaged in a strategic planning project with an immersive learning company. They focused on teaching empathy in health care environments in response to malpractice lawsuits. The financial exposure the risk of malpractice introduces to insurance companies, hospitals, and physicians' practices has resulted in extensive, scientific research into the reasons why people sue. We tapped into this research as part of our planning process and what we discovered was very surprising. It turns out people sue based upon how they feel they were treated after a medical error had occurred and not directly because of the error itself. Patients and patients' families that were treated with empathy were significantly less likely to sue. That's a powerful statement. In the midst of experiencing one of the most severe health and emotional crisis humans may encounter, empathy was the balm that soothed the intensity of a catastrophic medical event. Imagine the power empathy can have in an everyday business environment!

The third definition of authenticity is "undisputed credibility", which emphasizes the importance of being impeccable with your word and ensuring the consistent alignment of your actions with your words. Walking the walk and talking the talk. In the noble words of St. Francis of Assisi, "It is no use walking anywhere to preach unless our walking is our preaching."

One of the fastest ways to disengage a workforce is for leadership to display behavior that is inconsistent with their words. It conveys the existence of double standards; one for associates and a separate, privileged set of standards for executives. If you want associates to perform at a high level then live, work, and consistently display that level in your own behavior. Keep in mind it is human nature to remember the missteps. You can be consistently credible 99% of the time but it will be the one time you are inconsistent with your word that associates will remember.

Another powerful, yet often overlooked attribute of authentic leadership is the ability to sense and respect people's boundaries. Hierarchical leadership has a tendency to create boundaries that run in one direction. Actually, they are more like barriers than boundaries. Barriers that create a set of expectations that govern behavior and one-directional communication that are meant to sustain authority and control. Projecting a lack of respect for the boundaries of subordinates causes emotional barriers to be erected. As emotional barriers come up associate engagement goes down. Conversely, enabling the creation of healthy boundaries engages associates' sense of worth and creativity.

People need to feel secure in their own space; this extends to emotional and intellectual space as well as physical space. When people are able to create and maintain a *container of self* their creativity will blossom. When physical space is constrained, such as when cubicles are used for workspace, fostering healthy emotional and mental boundaries is even more important to fully engage associates. Authority figures that roll over these boundaries lead people to freeze up and withdraw, working while *keeping their heads down* to avoid further transgressions into their comfort zone. Giving associates the space to think and, at the appropriate time, to simply be, engages the imagination and the heart. The consistent expression of authentic leadership will rapidly reveal previously unseen opportunities for the organization.

~ Enlightened Strategic Planning

When I was a young executive working in Corporate America, I began to experience something that, at the time, I couldn't quite explain. As I was given responsibility to create or turn around business units, I would always start by sitting down with my front-line managers and field associates to discuss where we were, what internal and external challenges were before us, and solicit their opinions as to what we should do to move the business forward. I felt strongly that by taking an inclusive approach I would begin to gain their trust and best serve the interests of the company by embracing the experience and day-to-day knowledge of what was really happening in the trenches. We would then embark on the strategic planning process during which time we would openly challenge our assumptions in lively discourse and stretch the boundaries of what was traditionally perceived to be possible. From this process a momentum would emerge, more rapidly and more powerfully than what any of us could have imagined!

I had come to appreciate that the strategic planning process was an iterative one, and the questions that we asked of ourselves were often more important than the answers we would eventually discover. Upon reaching agreement on the plan of action, I would travel to the field to communicate the vision and strategy that we had developed, again drawing the associates into a lively conversation of what was and wasn't working. I emphasized we had a shared responsibility to ensure we were taking care of our customers and embracing the spirit of our strategic plan. I would continuously remind everyone that the strategic plan was a living document, it was not etched in stone, and everyone was empowered to help calibrate the implementation of the plan moving forward.

The one constant that I began to observe surprised me. At the point in time that we had perhaps fifty to sixty percent of our strategies implemented we would be on track to achieve our objectives! It seemed illogical to me at first. How could we be tracking 100% to plan when we were only half way through the implementation and execution of our strategies? What I know now is that I was observing the power of collective intention, the cumulative energy that accelerated the manifestation of our vision! This energy was a direct result of the culture we had co-created. A culture that was kindled by the intention and creative visualization that was expressed through the strategic planning process (we will explore this further in step-by-step detail in Chapter Seven).

The concept of employing creative visualization as the first step in manifesting a new reality is not new. Our intention helps us create a wondrous reality that we, as spiritual beings, are meant to enjoy. On the surface it may sound a bit *New Age* to some people, a bit beyond the pale of what we, as Westerners, consider realistic.

Yet haven't we all observed a similar occurrence that is very common in athletics? We have all heard a broadcaster covering a football or basketball game suddenly exclaim how one of the teams has all the *momentum*. We cannot see the force behind the momentum yet we can observe its effects on the game. Suddenly, through a shift in attitude and energy everything seems to fall into place for one of the teams. In a matter of a few plays, one team is more dynamic than the other, and their execution becomes so well orchestrated the other team almost looks as if they are standing still trying to defend them. A quarterback or point guard is suddenly *in the zone*, their timing is in perfect alignment with their teammates, they're somehow anticipating the defense...they just can't miss. The announcer exclaims, "They're really feeling it now!" It is the exact same phenomena I was witnessing in business.

Athletics offer us a wonderful example of presence, which is a core attribute of conscious leadership, of being totally present in the moment, in the now. An Olympic gymnast is not thinking about all the details of a routine as they perform. A golfer cannot be thinking about the nuances of mechanics during his or her swing. They quiet their minds and enter into a near meditative state as they compete. They are conscious of their performance but not thinking about their performance. Athletes, when at the top of their game anticipate and act rather than think and react.

This phenomena is supported by hard science. When we are fully engaged and enjoying what we are doing we enter what renowned researcher and psychology professor Mihaly Csikszentmihalyi refers to as *flow*. Dr. Csikszentmihalyi's research looked into the psychological state of a wide variety of professionals operating at peak performance. When they were fully engaged, focused, and enjoying their endeavor, their biochemistry reflected an increase in cortisol (part of the hypothalamic/pituitary/ adrenal or HPA axis in our brains) which brought them to a place in which they were taking full advantage of their cognitive and physical abilities. If the HPA axis shot past this optimal point due to stress, adrenaline and cortisol levels continued to rise and performance rapidly diminished. His work proved that a person's emotional state is a governing factor in cognitive and physical performance.

When a group of athletes are engaging in team competition (and doing it well) they manifest a cumulative energy. Their combined intention, their collective consciousness, elevates the team to an entirely new level of performance. We can achieve the same thing in business; fore it is not simply physical or mental execution but the collective consciousness of our team that generates this remarkable energy. The key is in creating a strategic plan and dynamic culture that empowers our associates to be present in the moment, to concentrate on creating and delivering value to our customers now, rather than being consumed with what may come tomorrow or concerned about what wasn't done yesterday.

Strategic planning as a form of creative visualization that also enables presence may raise the question, "How are you in the moment when you are looking one, three, or five years ahead?" It is a logical question. Let me use an analogy to help explain this:

Let's envision a business, just for a moment, as a tribe of hunters and gatherers living ten thousand years ago. As the leaders of the tribe, we are highly aware of our environment. As time passes, we begin to observe a change in the climate; with each passing year it is getting colder much earlier in the year and staying cold much longer into the spring. We observe the birds and other animals beginning to migrate south much earlier than what we have historically observed and notice they are also returning later in the spring. From our observations, from our awareness, we develop a Vision that these elongated winters may be less severe in the South. It stands to reason that if the migrating animals are leaving earlier and staying longer food supplies are most likely more abundant as well.

We establish a Goal of migrating south to ensure the tribe will continue to prosper. In order to do so, we must cross a large mountain range before the early autumn snows begin and block the high passes. We now have an Objective that is critical to the success of achieving our Goal; we must clear the high passes before the snow flies or we could become stranded and perish.

There are many passes we can choose from, some representing a more arduous climb, but are more direct, and others that offer a gentle slope, yet will take longer. We must now decide upon our Strategies. The amount of risk we are willing to incur and how we intend to balance the risk of each approach with the risk of failing to reach the passes before the snows begin.

Our Strategies reflect the constraints we have identified through a thorough Self-Assessment. We have examined our strengths and weaknesses. How many children and elders must survive this trek? Do we have ample supplies for the journey? Who are our harbingers for this journey that can blaze the trail for the remainder of the tribe? Have we carefully evaluated the landscape and challenged our assumptions of the risks involved? What is the Competitive Landscape; are there hostile tribes living along the way that may wish us harm? Might there be opportunities to partner with other tribes? Have we properly scouted our options and truly know what we face? Have we challenged our assumptions and appreciate the fact we still don't know what we don't know?

At the end of all this discussion and evaluation we realize that the only way we can manifest our Vision (abundance for the tribe) and achieve our Goal (to be in the South), and to secure our Objective (navigate the mountain passes before the autumn snow), is to walk south every day one step at a time, regardless of the Strategic path we have chosen. Our Tactics...for each of us, once the decision has been made to take the journey, must simply focus on taking one step at a time in the moment.

Much like the tribal elders in this analogy, business leaders have the responsibility of formulating a clear and concise vision, communicate it effectively so that others can share in it, and to discern the best path for the organization to follow through the mature evaluation of risks and rewards. In doing so, we can, in combination with a healthy, vibrant, and trusting culture, enable associates to concentrate on each step they are taking in the moment, to be truly present, to execute on the plan now and make it a reality for us all.

~ Creative Culture

While leadership is paramount in orchestrating the creative visualization of an enlightened strategic planning process, it is the propagation of culture that will carry an organization forward to scalable heights (or lows; it cuts both ways) that resonate far beyond a single personality. It is much like the relationship between a gardener and their garden. The gardener may be capable of inspirational work, but it is the garden that inspires.

The traditional definition of organizational culture is the shared values, norms, artifacts, and embraced behaviors of an enterprise. This is a somewhat superficial definition that historically has proven to poorly serve leaders attempting to drive performance or organizational change. At best, it places culture at the periphery of the company, as if it is a side effect of the mission. At worst, by referring to culture as an artifact, it infers that the culture is a coincidental by-product or relic of the organization.

In reality, culture is the vibrational resonance of the collective consciousness of the organization. This immediately changes the way we think about culture. It is no longer a by-product of what a company does but a powerful force that affects everything and everybody involved in the business. The frequency of cultural energy is self-generating and perpetually regenerating. When we drop a pebble into a pool we cannot alter the ripples that move continuously outward without disrupting the entire pool. It is leadership's role to drop the appropriate pebbles, at the appropriate time, knowing the resonance will expand beyond their immediate control.

For nearly a decade working as a strategic consultant with life science and medical device start-up enterprises I began to notice a common challenge shared by these companies. The vast majority of these companies emerge from intellectual property cultivated in academic settings. As these companies are formed they bring along members of the research staff and are often lead by a scientist, physician, or engineer that first developed the technology in their laboratory. It is an exciting time reflecting the natural progression of organizational evolution, but this progression requires substantive, adaptive change at the very heart of the enterprise.

Unwittingly, these entrepreneurs bring along the academic culture from whence they came. The culture that was ideal for the nurturing and early cultivation of their intellectual property is ironically very poorly suited for the business environment they are attempting to enter. This is exacerbated by the nature of their technology and the critical demands of customers, regulators, and investors in the health care and pharmaceutical research markets. The mission has changed (moving from creating technology to commercializing technology) yet the emerging organization clings to their historical culture, usually quite unaware of the risk this is about to introduce to the nascent company.

I've observed that these start-up companies are often unaware of the imperative need to quickly migrate from an academic culture to that of a business oriented culture. This naiveté is a leading contributor of failure in early stage companies. It is not the technology that fails; it is leadership's inability to recognize the significance of culture and the fundamental importance of creating and cultivating the culture necessary to meet the high expectations of their target marketplace.

But why is this? These are quite often remarkably gifted intellectuals capable of remarkable discoveries, insights, and performance. It is a facet of business dogma that culture is a by-product of artifacts, shared values, and attitudes rather than the actual energy of the collective consciousness of the organization. It is not peripheral; it is concentric to the very essence of the organization.

The academic culture to which they cling isn't bad; it is just as it should be in the early, creative stages of intellectual property. It simply no longer resonates with the frequency the evolving organization needs to successfully connect with customers in a commercial environment. The very nature of the enterprise has evolved and it is leadership's responsibility to anticipate and ignite the new energy and intention necessary to fulfill this new mission.

One of the reasons culture may be perceived as an allusive, almost amorphous issue may be due to the fact that it is rarely discussed during the early stages of company creation. There are so many urgent and demanding issues organizations face as they struggle to establish traction and stability in the marketplace. Culture always seems to take a back seat in development. From my experience, it is only when culture becomes a problem that there is a conscious effort to address the situation. By that time it is like trying to turn around an aircraft carrier traversing the Suez Canal. The constraints of the business make it a formidable task that no one wants to get in front of in order to resolve.

Another reason business culture tends to take on a seemingly uncontrolled life of its own is the lack of focus on culture in the development and execution of the strategic plan. It simply isn't a traditional core focus of senior management and it can be a difficult area to measure in an objective manner. Perhaps industrial companies operating in the twentieth century could get away with ignoring this strategic imperative, but contemporary enterprises leveraging intellectual property for value creation can no longer afford to avoid the importance of culture.

The propagation of a creative, healthy culture begins with the expressed intention of authentic leadership. Associates take their cue from the words and behaviors of their executives. If leadership expresses a predatory, *win at all cost* philosophy, the behaviors of the organization will follow suit. Nowhere is the old adage of reaping what one sows more accurately reflected than in the creation of organizational culture. When associates buy-in to the vision, intention, and strategy, a corresponding, positive energy begins to resonate throughout a business. As a business grows in size, the outer bands of this energy are subject to the laws of inertia. A body at rest tends to stay at rest and a body in motion tends to stay in motion. This is why culture demands attention early in the developmental stages of a business. Once the initial, framing forces are unleashed they are very difficult to modulate.

The traditional definition of culture references shared values; this warrants a bit more discussion. Culture is affected by the shared, living values of an organization.

There are two types of living values in a company; explicit shared values and implicit shared values.

Explicit values are best reflected through thoughtfully crafted Vision Statements and Mission Statements. These formal articulations define who we are and where we're going. Unfortunately, these formal statements are often another area of peripheral focus, especially in emerging organizations (we'll discuss creating powerful Vision and Mission Statements in detail in Chapter Six). Explicit values are also reinforced through the language and focus expressed in standard operating procedures. This emphasizes how we will act in the daily conduct of our business; how we will treat our customers and stakeholders and resonate with the sense of responsibility we have to those working around us.

Explicit values are almost always highly positive in their intention but they can be dramatically tempered by the implicit values of an organization. These are the *unwritten rules* of a company and these unspoken values are capable of derailing the finest intentions.

Implicit values often emerge from ego and therefore are frequently based in fear, insecurity, and the desire to perpetuate positions of power. Unwritten rules can cover a wide spectrum of acceptable and non-acceptable behaviors in a company. Expectations of dress, informal lines of communication throughout the hierarchy, subtle power influencers, and the evaluation criteria of performance are prime examples. I've even experienced environments where the exercising of vested stock options was perceived to be a career killer by senior management! This certainly wasn't written anywhere, but it was clearly understood by everyone.

The example we've probably all experienced at one time or another is the existence of a *good ole' boy network* in a company. The existence of such cliques are, by definition, *exclusive*, rather than inclusive. They disenfranchise talented associates and propagate office politics. Such cliques often display passive aggressive behaviors that exist only to serve the ego and selfish desires of individuals in an organization.

The consistent display of authentic leadership helps ensure the alignment of implicit values with organizational intention. This makes sense as authentic leadership is not rooted in the ego. Authentic leadership also cultivates empathy throughout the culture, a powerful and binding force of positive intention. We'll explore this in more detail in Chapter Eight.

It is impossible to parse out any one of the three key attributes of transformational performance. They are all intertwined in the tapestry of the organization and require continuous attention over time. With these concepts as our backdrop we can now begin to discuss the step-by-step process to transform your organization or lay the right foundation for your startup endeavor!

~ Key Concepts

- Strategic planning is a form of creative visualization which cultivates presence.
- Organizational culture resonates the frequency of collective consciousness.
- Execution is driven by the authenticity of leadership.
- All three aspects must be attended to in order to spark transformational performance.

The Transformational Entrepreneur

Chapter Three ~ The Power of Vision and Intention

"Your vision will become clear only when you look into your heart ... Who looks outside, dreams. Who looks inside, awakens." Carl Jung

A clear and impassioning vision can change the world. The seminal political, social, economic, scientific, and spiritual movements throughout the history of humankind can often be traced to a single, inspiring vision. A vision of an unforeseen reality, held by a lone human being, with unquestioning resolve, is capable of delivering dramatic improvements to the human condition. Vision is the seed of change. Yet vision requires germination, and it is the intention held by the visionary that determines, to a great extent, its growth and adoption throughout the greater community.

I've had the good fortune to have worked as a senior executive for a company that espoused an inspiring vision based upon the development of a revolutionary technology. It was an advance so dramatic that at first it was an affront to the medical, scientific, and business dogma of the day. It was the epitome of a disruptive technology; something that would create an entirely new method heretofore unseen and unanticipated in the marketplace. On a separate occasion I was the senior sales executive at a company that had developed a technology just as remarkable, just as promising, but lacked the intention necessary to successfully bring it to market. There were lessons of enormous value in both experiences worth discussing.

In the 1980's a gentleman by the name of H. William Hillebrenner[8] came up with a concept for rapidly sterilizing heat-sensitive, surgical endoscopes that were enabling the emergence of minimally invasive surgical procedures. At the time, Mr. Hillebrenner was working for the American Sterilizer Company (AMSCO) in Erie, PA.

These endoscopes allow surgeons to make a small incision in the patient rather than opening up the entire abdomen. This minimized the risk of infection, dramatically shortened recovery times, lowered health care costs, and contributed dramatically to positive patient

---

[8] The following individuals were contributors to the development of the technology and are listed on the patent for the STERIS System 1® - H. William Hillebrenner, Vipul B. Sheth, Joseph M. Stack, Charles T. Curtis, Kevin H. Butler, David E. Shoff, Robert S. Petko, William C. Little, Thaddeus Mielnik, and Peter Zell.

outcomes. At the time, the primary method of sterilization, the use of steam under pressure, would destroy the scopes, so the instruments had to be sterilized using gas. This took a minimum of twenty-four hours to reprocess. This time consuming turnaround between procedures combined with the high expense of the scopes limited the number of minimally invasive surgeries hospitals could perform.

Mr. Hillebrenner's concept was roundly dismissed by AMSCO's leadership; after all, they manufactured steam and gas sterilizers and had dominated the U.S. market for nearly one hundred years. Why would they want to cannibalize their own sales for this seemingly outlandish concept that, in their opinion, would most likely never even work? Mr. Hillebrenner and AMSCO parted company, and from the stories, in less than magnanimous fashion.

It looked as if this revolutionary technology would be lost to the ages until it came to the attention of a private equity group in neighboring Ohio. They commissioned an executive by the name of Bill Sanford to investigate the technology. Mr. Sanford had twenty years of experience in the medical device industry and was managing his own consulting firm at the time. He met with Mr. Hillebrenner to evaluate the technology which was based upon a cold chemical process integrated with a device that would flush the lumens and sterilize both the internal and external surfaces of an endoscope.

Mr. Sanford determined there were limitations to the existing chemistry, but the vision of being able to sterilize flexible endoscopes within the operating room in less than thirty minutes captivated his imagination. He saw how this system could revolutionize health care by enabling the widespread adoption of minimally invasive surgical techniques. Based upon Bill Sanford's vision, the investors provided one million dollars and hired Bill to run the new company they formed to bring this technology to fruition. STERIS® Corporation was born.

Bill Sanford had an unrelenting vision, but he didn't stop there. He developed the foundations of a transformational organizational culture. He personally took every opportunity to preach the tenets of this culture to any that would listen. We associates all knew the central tenet word for word, "No activity, other than safety on the job, was more important than taking care of the Customer." Yes, customer was a formal noun in our world, and we all understood why this was so. Bill's passion became our passion. Each and every day we knew we were fighting the good fight, making significant contributions to health care that were improving the human condition. His vision expanded over time to encompass a systemic approach to infection prevention throughout the entire health care delivery system on a global scale.

Within a few short years STERIS Corporation purchased AMSCO. The technology that was so casually dismissed by the short sighted leadership of a complacent, entrenched organization had emerged to create a market value of the start-up company so significant that it was able to buy a company more than five times its size.

Bill Sanford's vision, intention, and appreciation of corporate culture had parleyed a million dollar investment and a technology that didn't quite work at the time into a company worth more than one billion dollars on the New York Stock Exchange in a dozen years. His vision ignited the rapid, global evolution of minimally invasive surgery into the standard of care for dozens of procedures. These procedures saved untold millions of dollars in health care expenditures while alleviating a myriad of human suffering. Bill Sanford's vision and intention changed the world.

My experience working on the other side of the coin was with a company (that will go nameless) that owned the rights to one of the most significant improvements in freezing technology in the history of the life sciences. Rather than forcing cold onto a sample, the technology actually removed latent heat so quickly ice crystals didn't have a chance to form within the cells.

We've all forgotten a glass bottle of some sort of liquid in the freezer and subsequently had to clean up the mess when the liquid expanded as ice formed and the bottle burst. The same thing happens when freezing biological samples; as the water within the cells form ice crystals they expand and burst the cellular walls and a significant portion of the sample is no longer biologically viable.

The president of the company, to whom I reported, believed this was an enabling technology that would empower remarkable breakthroughs in stem cell research, artificial reproductive technology, and a variety of other life science applications.

It was especially promising for the preservation of human oocytes (unfertilized eggs) for women diagnosed with cancer that face therapies that render them infertile. At the time embryos (a fertilized egg) could be frozen, but young women that did not have a partner had no way of preserving their fertility when facing chemotherapy.

Preliminary research with the oocyte application had proven highly promising. I felt that this advancement had the potential of helping young women facing a life threatening illness maintain a positive attitude of survival and for living a complete, fulfilling life upon recovery. It might provide an additional bit of hope that could be the difference between life and death.

What should have been another exciting and noteworthy success story proved to be painfully disappointing. The president's vision was one of control and greed. It lacked empathy for the human condition and the absence of any measure of altruism doomed the business from the very start. He would not sell the device, but would only rent it and license the technology. He had a vision of "reaching through" with the licensing of the technology into areas of value creation that were, in effect, well beyond our contribution. The president could not be dissuaded from his stranglehold approach and a year after entering the life science market not a single unit had been placed. The once hopeful promise of this technology withered away on the vine. His intention was self-serving and the negativity this projected came right back to the organization.

A leader's vision is empowered by intention. Cultivating a vision that goes beyond basic profitability brings a greater energy and purpose to the organization. Profitability is, of course, paramount. It sustains the business and enables the delivery of value to its customers, shareholders, and stakeholders. Without it there isn't a business for very long. A vision that solely focuses on money, however, eventually fails to inspire the collective consciousness of the organization and marketplace. STERIS offered a vision with a high degree of altruism and the company blossomed. The freezing technology company offered a vision of control, expressed no concern for improving the human condition, and failed miserably. The intention of vision matters.

The clarity of vision is also significant. Leaders should ask themselves, "Is my vision tangible and easily understood?" The use of basic language that communicates a concrete outcome that anyone can appreciate and embrace will quickly inspire those who hear the message.

A great example was President Kennedy's vision of placing a man on the moon within a decade. Everyone that heard this could visualize the result by simply looking up into the night sky. If he had expressed his intention by explaining the importance of successfully competing with the Soviet Union for dominance in near-earth space exploitation it probably wouldn't have had the same effect with the public.

Another presidential initiative that delivered a far greater impact on the lives and well-being of Americans was President Nixon's "War on Cancer". This sparked the remarkable growth in federally funded research at the National Institutes of Health which now approaches thirty billion dollars annually. Nixon's vision of battling disease was much more conceptual than visual. While the tangible, humanitarian results of Nixon's initiative are arguably much greater than the results of the Apollo program it was also far less inspirational. Nearly every child of my generation wanted to be an astronaut, but not too many of us dreamed of becoming molecular biologists.

The resonance of vision is amplified by the unwavering commitment of leadership. It is the missionary zeal of leadership that propels a business towards success. Passion is a powerful energy that will draw like-minded, like-hearted professionals into the fold. It can attract the capital a company requires to invest in growth. It can secure the early adopters, the first customers an enterprise needs to gain traction when entering a new market. Passion, in effect, broadcasts the value and inspirational message of vision to the entire spectrum of constituents a company requires to succeed. Jack Welch, the fabled CEO of General Electric summed up the relationship between leadership and vision, "Good business leaders create a vision, articulate the vision, passionately own the vision, and relentlessly drive it to completion."

The source of vision can come from many directions, inputs, and influences but it always aligns with a leader's intuition. Vision must not only look right, it must feel right. Ask yourself a question; have you ever been passionate for something or someone when it didn't feel intuitively correct?

Passion is not rooted in the intellect, it comes from the heart. It is a feeling that, from outside observation, often overpowers what we assume to be the rational path of avoiding challenging constraints and seemingly insurmountable barriers. When we know something is intuitively correct, and we trust in ourselves, we are unshakable...we know, we believe in our ability to change the world regardless of the odds! People that lack vision are unfortunately trapped within a world of their own mental constraints. Visionary leaders are already living in a new reality...they're simply the first ones in the room!

On the surface it may appear to many that there is no place for intuition in the business world. This attitude is especially common in the West. After all, responsible business decisions should be made rationally based upon a thorough analysis of well researched and validated facts. While this is undoubtedly important, it discounts the full capacity of the human continuum. Human beings are so much more than just rational thought. Discounting our intuition, especially when cultivating vision, is like playing piano with one hand. The melody might be pretty, but there can be no harmony.

Recent advances in the emerging disciplines of neurocardiology and neurogastroenterology support the premise that intelligence resides in the body as well as in the brain. Our gastrointestinal system has more than 100 million neurons, more than the entire spinal cord. Research by developmental biologists indicate this "gut brain", called the enteric system, forms in the embryo when a small clump of neural cells splits and migrates to what will become the brain and the gastrointestinal system. The enteric system is capable of expressing critical neurotransmitters such as dopamine, serotonin, norephinephrine, and glutamate much in the same way as the brain.

The heart also has neural cells with similar capabilities. As we develop in utero, these neural networks are eventually connected by the vagus nerve. While the vagus nerve enables communication, each neural network is capable of autonomous function. There is an inherent truth in the old sayings "his heart wasn't in it" and "going with your gut". What we refer to as intuition may, in fact, emerge from these other *brains*. Research is just discovering the ability of our bodies to process information and input from sources we may not be cognitive of in our head.

Adding to the challenge we modern humans have in embracing our intuitive messages is the fact that the vagus nerve connects to the brain at the basal ganglia. This ancient part of our brain has no direct neural pathways to the higher parts of our brain that process language. Contemporary humans are enamored by our faculty of speech. It dominates our thinking and perceptions of the world. Lacking the tags of language, the messages, or *feelings* we receive from our embodied neural network tend to be discounted in our mental prioritization of thought. The fact is, however, when we are connected to these centers, when our hearts, minds, and guts are aligned by intention we emit a radiance capable of connecting and inspiring those around us!

In his book, "The Other 90%" Robert Cooper discusses the importance of how these other neural centers in our bodies enable the human experience. "In terms of human ingenuity and initiative, it also turns out that the heart is not only open to new possibilities, it actively scans for them, ever seeking new intuitive understanding of what matters most to you in your life or work."[9] He adds that the heart's electromagnetic field "is approximately 5,000 times greater than the field produced by the brain."[10] Mr. Cooper goes on to reference a study from the Center for Creative Leadership that concluded, "the only statistically significant factor differentiating the very best leaders from the mediocre ones is caring about people. It's not that we don't need a foundation of other qualities and competencies to

---

[9] "The Other 90%", Robert Cooper, Three Rivers Press, New York, NY, 2001, p. 17.

[10] Ibid, p. 17.

work well in a given field. It's that caring is the glue that holds all this together and enables people to shine." [11]

I've experienced this first-hand while studying with Linda Kohanov[12] at the Epona International Study Center in Arizona. Linda, a celebrated author and expert in Equine Facilitated Experiential Learning, works with horses to facilitate personal and professional development.

In her work, Linda reveals that as prey animals, horses are highly sensitive to their environment. Their large guts and hearts radiate bands of energy that sense the presence and intention of other beings approaching their physical space. Through her years of work with her Black Horse Herd, Linda has also come to understand that horses process emotions as information, without judgment, and act accordingly. As such, horses are remarkably sensitive reflective mirrors for humans; enabling experiential insights to emerge from within that contribute to emotional intelligence, self-awareness, and presence.

While conducting round pen exercises with the horses at Epona I experienced these phenomena of connection and

---

[11] Ibid, p. 18.

[12] I recommend Linda Kohanov's book, "Riding Between The Worlds", available through New World Library, Novato, CA.

cooperation. When I entered the round pen grounded in my body and with authentic intention the horse *joined up* with me. The horse moved with me around the pen without my saying a word or touching them. If I entered the pen while being *in my head,* or with misaligned or masked intention, the horse wanted nothing to do with me.

It isn't a coincidence that many of the greatest leaders of history were also great horse people. Alexander the Great, Joan of Arc, George Washington, even Ronald Reagan were all phenomenal with people as well as horses! It is the authenticity of self combined with noteworthy intention that enables a powerful connection to emerge with horses as well as people...of leading from the heart and spirit as well as from the head.

Intention from the heart cannot be masked, it eventually comes to the surface. People can feel this, but contemporary society has led us towards a rationalism that discounts other sources of knowing. The embodiment of vision and authentic intention creates an infectious passion that resonates with everyone you encounter. Its impact on success in business cannot be overstated.

~ Key Concepts

- Intention Resonates – Vision needs to encompass more than making money. A vision that resonates with an altruistic intention will attract similar energy in the form of resources, customers, and associates. Intention matters.

- Clarity Communicates – Express your vision in tangible terms. Tell it as a story. The more people that can easily relate to and understand your vision, the more powerful it becomes.

- Passion Amplifies – Passion is infectious. It amplifies the energy of intention and positive intention attracts similar intention. Passion ignites and motivates.

- Intuition Validates – Do your homework and then listen to your gut. To quote Albert Einstein, "The only real valuable thing is intuition. The intellect has little to do on the road to discovery."

~ Exercise

Write a short story about the successful manifestation of your vision. Write it as if the business has already achieved an unparalleled level of success. If you're having trouble getting started, imagine you are answering questions for an interview to be published in a major business publication. Here are some sample questions you can answer and expound upon:

- How did it all get started?
- What is it about your company that has differentiated you in the market and contributed to such rapid growth?
- What were the hurdles early on that challenged the company? What did the organization learn from navigating those difficult times?
- I've read you attribute a great deal of your success to your associates. How do you attract and retain such a high level of talent?
- What's next? Where do you see the company growing from here?

The Transformational Entrepreneur

Chapter Four ~
Self-Awareness and the Self-Assessment

"He who knows others is wise; he who knows himself is enlightened." Lao-Tzu

Armed with your vision, you are now ready to begin the strategic planning process for your business. The process embarks with the Self-Assessment, which on the surface may appear to be a relatively simple step. It can and it should be, but its ease is contingent on the maturity of leadership. The effectiveness of the Self-Assessment is directly proportional to the level of leadership's self awareness. Before conducting the Self-Assessment for the business, leadership will be greatly served by undertaking an assessment of its self.

We can all agree that engaging our minds in our daily business practices is a fundamentally sound practice. However, garnering our image of self, of who we are in our essence, from the perceptions of our mind, is an illusion based upon learned behavior, fear, and regret. How often do we find our minds consumed with an inner conversation of "what ifs", worrying about a future that, in reality, may never come to pass? A future that in reality does not yet exist. Or conversely, how often do we expend emotional energy lamenting a lost love, a career misstep, or a perceived mistake from the historic path of our lives? Again, the past is no more a reality than the future. They are projections of our mind.

We can only be, only act, in the present. Being fully engaged in the moment, to have presence, is one definition of being enlightened. It is the suspension of the ego, of the perception our mind has as to who and what we are within the context of how our society has conditioned our behavior. Of putting the cacophonous conversation the mind is having with itself to rest, freeing one's self from the illusion of past and future and existing in the only true reality we have; this present moment. When we do so, we become aware of the infinite essence of who we actually are; a sense of our true self emerges from the stillness that washes over us with the quieting of the ego-driven mind. This also places us in close proximity with our intuition, the perennial wisdom that resides within us all.

As a business leader and long-time executive I have observed that most of the strife, energetic drain, and unproductive behavior expressed within the work place emerges from the constant conflict of ego-driven minds careening off of one another. Managing within such an environment is like trying to play pinball with a dozen balls on the table at once. You eventually get flipper fatigue!

Such environments often cultivate passive aggressive behavior, which is a value destroyer that foments an endless cycle of resentment, guarded behavior, and partial effort. It disengages the surrounding talent from being fully present and contributing on a daily basis. Unfortunately, we've probably all witnessed and experienced similar environments where the leadership actually rewards, either consciously or unconsciously, this exact behavior.

This is where the authenticity of leadership sets the tone for the entire organization. A business leader that is disingenuous cannot expect anything but the same negative energy in return from their associates. The leader sets the standard, the behavioral expectations that will resonate throughout the company's collective consciousness and resulting culture. We spoke earlier of authenticity being rooted in being true to one's self, a manifestation of presence, of enlightenment. Authenticity is more of a process than a place, a continuous path of spiritual growth and awareness. There are many ways of placing one's footsteps upon this path.

The single most powerful method for quieting the chattering mind is through meditation. There are many excellent books and audio programs that are available on meditation that can assist us in finding the stillness within us that is the fountainhead of the true self. Modern medicine also recognizes the many health benefits that emerge through meditative practice. You will find most methods remarkably similar. Some may work better for you than others and it can be fun to experiment with the different approaches until you find one that best suits you. The intent of mediation is to suspend cognitive thought in order to elevate your awareness of conscious being. This practice opens a path to your true self, your eternal self that is one with the energy of all Creation.

If you are unfamiliar with the practice, here is a simple approach to meditation. Find a time and place in which you will not be disturbed. Place a cushion on the floor and sit upon it with your back straight but not rigid. You can also try this laying down, what is important is to be comfortable. Rest your hands upon your lap and relax your neck, shoulders, and face. Bring your attention to where you are. Listen to the sounds around you, find your body, find your breath. Focus on your breathing, relaxing with each exhalation. Pay attention to your incoming and outgoing breathing. Quiet your mind. If you find your mind wandering off, into thought, bring your attention gently back to your breath.

It is important to be patient as you embark along your path of meditation. At first it will be somewhat difficult to suspend the conversation in your mind. When I first started meditating I would sit and focus on my breath, struggling to get my brain to shut up! I would meditate for an hour, an hour and a half, and finally experience a wisp of absolute stillness, lasting perhaps only a second or two. The bliss I experienced in that fleeting moment was beyond joy, beyond the happiest feeling I have ever known. The more I meditate, the more I weave this practice into my daily life, the easier it is for me to attain this stillness, to experience the elation of pure being, of pure presence.

Another excellent method for cultivating presence is the body scan. I was first introduced to this concept by Linda Kohanov at the Epona Center. Prior to conducting reflective work with horses, participants in Linda's seminars conduct a body scan to establish an emotional and physical baseline. This is a simple centering practice bringing our awareness into the moment. The scan begins by standing still and taking notice to anything you feel in your body, such as tension, or any other sensation you may be aware of throughout your being.

The next step is to simply acknowledge the feeling, breathe into that place in your body, and ask it if it has any message for you. The first thing that comes to your mind is that message, the message from your mind-body (remember all those neural networks we spoke of in the last chapter). The body scan is repeated and, from what I've experienced and witnessed, the tension or feeling that was observed consistently dissipates.

By acknowledging and listening to the messages our bodies offer us, we align our embodied intelligence with our conscious mind. We become connected with the intelligence that exists within our entire being. We become fully congruent within our selves. Not only does this enable us to connect with horses, it also enables us to connect, on a thoroughly authentic level, with each other.

Researchers refer to this as *coherence*. It is a state in which people's pulse, blood pressure, and breathing align with one another as they connect in physical proximity.

There are other methods for tapping into the stillness of presence. Physical exertion can be very helpful. Yoga is an excellent example of physical exertion that centers the energy of being while quieting the mind. Some people find golf to be very Zen. Running on the beach or taking a long walk surrounded by the wonders of nature can also bring us closer to our true selves. Physical activity in combination with regular meditative practice will help develop inner balance and bring stillness closer to the surface of your everyday life.

The concept of tapping into stillness in order to ignite the activity of business may, at first, sound as if it is in juxtaposition. Allow me to share a metaphor. Our bodies are a vessel designed to support the spiritual self in this physical world. While our spirit resides in stillness, our bodies are beautifully designed for movement. Much like a sailboat, we can be remarkably splendid moored to the dock of our familiar, comfortable surroundings. But we are most wondrous when we are in motion, navigating our way to the discoveries of what is awaiting us over the horizon!

Even in motion, while underway, there is stillness to a sailboat. It moves in harmony upon the natural energy of the universe, consuming nothing, wasting nothing in its wake. The wind, driven by the radiational energy of the sun, fills our sails. The tides and currents, driven by the gravitational energy of the moon and the orbit of the earth, lap continuously at our hull. Once our course has been set and the most efficient tack determined, only minor adjustments, the smallest of effort need be expended at the helm and upon the sheets to continue upon our voyage. We are stillness in motion; in harmony with the energy of the universe. It is in this state of grace that our vessel can take us anywhere!

This is the state of conscious leadership, stillness in motion. The conscious leader is not motivated by fear or insecurities. They embrace their talents as well as their limitations, and by understanding their limitations they are able to surround themselves with complimentary talent that will be the warp in the tapestry of the business. The threads that add strength to the team. A leader must be self confident enough (in true self, not ego-driven confidence) to not only accept challenges from their associates, but to encourage everyone around them to challenge their assumptions.

When you create an environment that is healthy, trustworthy, and respectful, two significant attributes will emerge. First, you will attract the best of the best, people that have the talent your company needs combined with the proclivity towards spiritual awareness that will engage the entire spectrum of their human gifts. If you are present as a leader you will attract others that are equally present.

Second, you will begin to create a culture of honorable intention. The collective consciousness of the organization will be focused on serving the customer and community and not upon serving themselves. The associates that are drawn into the fold will inherently understand that if they do what is right by the customer, the rewards we all hope to attain will emerge. In starting the strategic planning process keeping these factors in mind will result in a realistic and relevant Self-Assessment.

If you discover an associate is displaying passive aggressive behavior, address it honestly and quickly, even if it is a star performer. Ignoring negative behavior is its own reward and the message this sends throughout the entire organization will resonate with a negative frequency that will disengage the good intentions of others in the company. One capable performer behaving badly can disrupt the culture you are seeking to cultivate. You should address the behavior (and be sure to isolate your concern on the behavior, not the person) with positive intention. Ask the associate if they are happy with what you are trying to create in the organization. Explain the vision and make sure they understand how what they are doing is disruptive to the goals of the team. It could be they've never been exposed to enlightened leadership and have been waiting to turn a corner themselves. Offer a path back into the fold and a timeframe for accomplishing the change. If a shift in behavior doesn't follow, counsel them on how you might help them find a situation elsewhere that would be more in line with their style. Remember, you can be firm and resolute while still being remarkably positive with your intention.

The Self-Assessment is fundamentally simple and straightforward. It is an assessment of the company's strengths, weaknesses, and core competencies and it is best initiated by employing a white-board session. Gather the planning team in front of a white-board and begin facilitating the conversation. This is a bit of an art in and of itself. It is important that you draw everyone into the conversation. If a member of the planning team is sitting quietly in the back of the room draw them into the discourse and ask their opinion of what is being said. The higher the degree of ownership that people feel at the outset of the strategic planning process will enhance the emerging value as you move into the more challenging facets of the process.

At the outset of the strategic planning process you should explain the intention of the exercise. Explain that it is an iterative process, meaning we will work through each step multiple times. It is a distillation of thought seeking greater clarity with each iteration of the process. Emphasize that at times, the questions the process forces us to ask of ourselves may in fact be more important than the answers. Collectively, as we embark on the process, we may not know all the answers, but we can be confident that by working together we can ask all the right questions.

Encourage the team not only to challenge their own assumptions, but to openly and aggressively challenge your assumptions. This can be a bit tricky at first. I have found that many associates do not come from organizations where they were encouraged to challenge the ideas of an authority figure. Be honest with them and explain this is the reason why they have been hired; to fully engage themselves in the process of moving the business forward towards success.

Explain how we owe it to each other and to our customers to find the right ways of thinking and doing things that build value for everyone. Challenging each other in an open and honest (not ego driven) manner will force us to greater levels of clarity and reveal perspectives that may not be native to everyone at the planning table.

The Self-Assessment should be a healthy exercise of the mind and spirit and it should not threaten the perceived value of anyone involved. It facilitates the entire group's path towards presence, towards the suspension of ego, and the enlightenment of the organization. It will also help tap into people's intuition and it will begin to enhance the collective consciousness of the enterprise.

~ Strengths, Weaknesses, and Core Competencies

The definition of strengths is obvious; things that the enterprise does well that deliver value to the customer. Conversely, weaknesses should also be obvious, but this area may require a bit more reflection and organizational soul-searching to espouse in a completely honest and open manner. It is like the old cliché interview question; we can all go on and on discussing our strengths, but who wants to delve into our weaknesses? This is where the suspension of the collective ego is so important. Emphasize this is not an exercise in judgment, but an attempt to identify and prioritize areas that may require additional investment and development in order to achieve the company's goals.

Differentiating between strengths and core competencies is a bit more challenging. You will most likely find yourself moving attributes from one category to the other repeatedly as you work through the debate. Here's the difference: Strengths are the things the organization does well which deliver value to the customer. Core competencies are strengths unique to the enterprise that deliver what many business strategists refer to as a continuous, competitive advantage in the marketplace. The traditional definition of continuous, competitive advantage is something that differentiates you in the eyes of your customers from your competition and keeps you several steps ahead of your competition.

Some companies cultivate a near maniacal focus on their competitors, often to their own detriment. A few years ago, FedEx® Office's performance was lagging after their acquisition of Kinko's. Much of the underperformance was attributed to the organization's failure in anticipating the rapid technological evolution in inexpensive, home office printing capabilities exacerbated by the downturn in the economy. I believe the misstep was strategic. FedEx appeared to be obsessed with UPS, and when UPS purchased Mail Boxes, Etc., FedEx felt compelled to counter this move by buying Kinko's. FedEx lost sight of their core competencies, the attributes that had built their brand equity in the marketplace. By being overly focused on maintaining their continuous, competitive advantage FedEx may have followed their competitor down the wrong road.

I believe there is a more constructive mindset to developing a continuous, competitive advantage. It is in creating a flourishing, preferential advantage. Language can be transformational in and of itself. It reflects and points to intention.

In my experience, I have found that companies that embrace the mantra of delivering a continuous, competitive advantage are often predatory cultures. The phrase itself focuses a disproportionate amount of negative, organizational energy on trying to outmaneuver the competition rather than focusing positive energy on supporting the customer. If your customer base prefers your value proposition it really doesn't matter what the competition is doing. This attitude doesn't profess being unaware of your competition, but points to paying attention to what actually delivers value to your company; serving the customer. A flourishing advantage also implies a growing advantage whereas a continuous advantage infers an uninterrupted sequence, neither growing nor diminishing. A small shift in language can have a remarkable impact on behavior.

Core competencies, when strategically leveraged, enable you to define and differentiate your position in the marketplace. They allow you to act in the best interest of your customers rather than react to the competition. They keep your competition on the defensive, off balance, and in a perceived position of the follower rather than the leader. One of the most powerful core competencies can be organizational intention. Not simply what you do in a market, but how you go about doing it.

~ Key Concepts

- The Self-Assessment begins with Self Awareness.
- Self Awareness is the first step towards cultivating enlightened leadership.
- The suspension of ego resonates through the organization's collective consciousness.

~ Exercise

Just for fun, conduct your own Self-Assessment.

STRENGTHS   **WEAKNESSES**

CORE COMPETENCIES

Chapter Five ~ Intuition and the Market Assessment

"There is no logical way to the discovery of these elemental laws. There is only the way of intuition, which is helped by a feeling for the order lying behind the appearance."
Albert Einstein

Having looked inward, you are ready to look outward into the marketplace to determine where your value proposition will enjoy the most success. In assessing the market you will want to explore your opportunities as well as your risks (also called threats), develop insight into the competitive dynamics you will face along the way, and anticipate any contingencies you may wish to develop in order to maintain a responsive, viable business.

Markets are a confluence of the dynamic energies and interactions of prospects, customers, partners, and competitors, often existing on a global scale. The key word today is dynamic. Markets are continuously moving, refining, dissipating, and reemerging based upon a multitude of influences affecting tastes, competitive imperatives, and perceptions of value. Markets have never moved faster and in today's world the window of opportunity opens and closes at unprecedented speed.

The natural lag in the traditional reporting of market information, whether from government agencies or private firms, introduces a measure of risk in the assessment of prospective business opportunities. Adding to this complexity is the remarkable deluge of information currently available to businesses. Paralysis by analysis has never been more likely to occur, or more threatening to the viability of a business strategy.

The incorporation of intuition can significantly accelerate your market assessment process. By initially cutting through the external noise of available information, your intuition can rapidly guide you towards successful positioning within the dynamic flow of competing opportunities.

Intuition taps into the ancient and perennial wisdom that resides within us all. The science of quantum physics has revealed that we, and everything that exists around us, are comprised of energy. Even matter of the highest density is mostly empty space resonating energy at a specific frequency. As conscious leaders we can align our authentic selves with the energetic flow that connects us with everything in Creation. The intelligence centers that reside within our bodies, our heart-mind and our gut, are naturally in tune with the matrix of energy and information that is the universe. Intuition is the calibration of our true selves with the true reality of existence. It is always present, we need only to listen, to tune in to our authentic selves, and trust in its voice.

The power of insight that comes through the trusting of our intuition is just that, a practice of allowing our selves to listen, to feel, and to trust in the sensation of what our being is attempting to tell us. Note the word "insight"; it infers looking within to secure a vision of clarity and perception that is inherently superior by definition. The same path that brings us to a place of conscious leadership will also place us firmly in touch with our intuition. It is found in the stillness that resides within us, in our authentic state of being.

The most common method for tapping into our intuition, even for those of us that are not actively conscious of it, is by *sleeping on it*. We have all been faced with complex situations or major decisions that we've put off for a day or two to allow ourselves to make a wise choice. That process clears space for us to listen to our heart and gut, to allow our intuition the chance to well up within us and guide us in the right direction. I think you will find that *sleeping on it* is a valuable practice during the assessment process; part of the reason the entire planning process is iterative in its nature.

As I have progressed as a business strategist I have gained a reputation for being somewhat visionary. For having acute foresight into the coming business trends. For having the ability to see how things may emerge slightly over the horizon. Looking back on my life I realize I have long trusted in my intuition.

The emergence of this trust was cultivated playing football as a teenager. Being less athletically gifted than the majority of the players around me, I had to anticipate what was going to occur before it happened in order to be a step ahead of the competition. I learned to look at formations while quickly assessing player tendencies, anticipating where the ball was going and how the movement of players would unfold. It was said I had a great *feel* for the game that enabled me to succeed on the playing field beyond what my basic athletic ability would have indicated.

After college I went into biotechnology sales where, being on my own in the field every day, I continued to depend on my intuition. I had to *read* highly sophisticated and intelligent prospects that were far beyond the manipulative sales techniques being taught at the time. Blindly attempting to pull a trial close on a Nobel laureate just didn't seem to be a good idea at the time! I had to trust in my intuition to know when I could close a deal or know when to back off and wait for a more appropriate time. I carried this trust of my gut as I ascended the corporate ladder and ventured off into the start-up world. It continues to serve me well to this day.

I will refrain from referencing, in detail, the documented, scientific studies of intuition in the decision making process. A quick Google Scholar® search will bring up more than 680,000 references of scientific studies into the subject of intuition. A quick canvassing of the research indicates successful entrepreneurs and executives are more highly in tune with their intuition than less successful business people. They follow their gut. It makes sense. Successful people are usually very confident in their own judgment and trust themselves above all others. I'm not sure if this confidence emerges from the egoic mind or through an enlightened perspective, but the net result is they are in tune with their intuition and adhere to their vision with missionary zeal.

Leveraging one's intuition is not only a viable end point in the assessment process, it is also a wonderful starting point. Many of the greatest scientific breakthroughs and technological inventions of humankind began with a hunch. Tapping into your intuition is a fantastic place to establish a hypothesis of your market opportunity. This approach has historically served me well in conducting market research.

I start with a hunch, a supposition, and begin to pursue my research to validate my intuitive assumption. I allow myself the luxury of wandering throughout the dense forest of information that is before us all, turning over stones, lifting foliage, seeking a glimpse of something that will captivate my heart and mind and resonate in my being. Quite often these wanderings bring me to places of new discoveries I had not yet contemplated, epiphanies I may have missed if I had taken a less circuitous path of investigation.

The internet is a fantastic place to begin your market research. While this sounds obvious in this day and age, let your intuition guide your investigation well beyond a keyword search engine approach. Wander around for a few hours and see where it takes you.

Trade associations are a great place to start. Associations often offer market research to members and non-members alike and it can be substantially more affordable than traditional market research reports.

Take the time to get to know the federal government resources that are available as well. You've already paid for these resources so you might as well take full advantage of them! You'll be amazed what you can learn by viewing public sites from the Department of Health and Human Services, the Department of Commerce, the U.S. Patent Office, and the Census Bureau.

Don't assume where you might find important information either. I have found incredible data on the U.S. market imbedded in research conducted by the Department of Commerce on foreign markets (The U.S. data was offered as a point of reference and comparison). Again, let your intuition guide you and give yourself the time to simply wander around. Go deep into search engine results. I've found fresh market data twenty to thirty pages into these searches.

Even if you can't afford private research, you'll find that most market research firms let you view their table of contents of reports for free. This can get you moving in directions you may not have thought of and lead you to additional resources that will help round out your initial investigation.

Your intuition can be a powerful divining rod. It will immerse you quickly and effectively into the research process and help keep you connected with all of your intelligence centers in your body and head.

A wonderful way to build trust with one's intuition is to integrate it with your opportunity assessments, to weave it into the fabric of your overall research and resulting segmentation. In a way it allows you to hedge your bet. Let your intuition guide the start of your research, gathering credible information as you move forward. The information you find will hone your vision and either validate or dismiss your intuitive assumptions. I think you'll be surprised at the strength of your intuitive direction.

Allow yourself the freedom to explore opportunities based upon what you feel as much as by what you think. Test your vision with potential prospects and gauge how they feel about your proposition as well as what they think about it. Now is the time to fly test balloons, to immerse yourself with your prospects and allow your heart to learn as much as your mind. Be open to where and how your value resonates in the marketplace.

A few years back I was asked to develop a market launch strategy for an advanced wound care product. The technology was based upon a highly innovative approach to healing open wounds. The primary challenge was the product was not yet a standard of care and therefore lacked the reimbursement coding necessary for payment from Medicare/Medicaid and major insurance companies.

The traditional path to market indicated the need for a professional standards strategy, recruiting the opinion leaders within this clinical specialty to build credibility and acceptance. This approach eventually leads to the device becoming a standard of care and the establishment of reimbursement coding to emerge. Within moments of reading the indication for use and the supporting clinical data my intuitive voice literally shouted "there's a faster and better way to go market...there are patients and clinicians that need this now"!

Listening further, my intuition led me to explore the financially hard-pressed environments of inner city, acute care hospitals. These hospitals are the health care delivery system of last resort for disenfranchised people that cannot access health insurance. Quite often, the emergency rooms of these hospitals are used in lieu of a primary care physician and the people depending on their care arrive with late-stage problems due to a lack of early intervention.

The demographic segments that depend on these hospitals also have an alarmingly high rate of diabetes. Diabetes requires vigilant daily care combined with regular clinical oversight that simply isn't affordable to many of these patients. Correspondingly high rates of complications occur that are associated with advanced stages of untreated diabetes. One of the most severe is the occurrence of foot ulcers that are notoriously difficult to heal due to the lack of circulation in the extremities. These sores can lay open for years and can lead to amputation, a devastating situation even for people that have access to the best health care available. The clinical research for the product indicated a high rate of efficacy in healing these wounds even in elderly patients.

The hospitals that were obligated to deliver care to these patients incurred exceptionally high costs associated with treatment. An early wound would immediately cost more than $5,000 to treat and this cost could rapidly escalate to more than $25,000. An amputation can cost more than $80,000 with less than $30,000 of that expense reimbursed by Medicare or Medicaid. Additional rehabilitation needs, post-amputation, rapidly brought the costs to well over $120,000! The hospitals, which are publicly owned non-profit organizations, are left to absorb more than two thirds of these expenses. The massive losses these hospitals incurred, combined with the critical need of the patients, offered substantial motivation to explore novel, affordable therapies even if the reimbursement wasn't yet in place. By listening to my intuition I was guided to the people most in need of the product, regardless of the perceived obstacle of standard of care status.

As you explore your potential opportunities you may find multiple market segments that have utility for your value proposition. This is especially common if you are commercializing intellectual property (i.e. software, professional services, telecommunications, life science technology, etc). Several years ago I was hired to develop a launch strategy for a revolutionary adult (not embryonic) stem cell platform. The developmental focus of the company had been on clinical applications but once again my intuitive voice told me the technology had a much higher value and a shorter path to market in the research and development world. As I began following the lead of my intuition my research indicated that even within the research and development segment there were at least five applications of utility (basic research, pharmaceutical screening, regenerative medicine, vectors, vaccines, etc.). There was an immediate need to prioritize the focus of the company as we launched the technology. In response to this need, I developed a decision matrix that integrated my market research as well as my intuition.

The prioritization decision process, which I called Dynamic Parallel Targeting®[13], establishes a baseline of comparative factors in order to measure common risk factors and costs against potential returns on investment. Some of the factors are hard data points and some of the factors are derived through intuition. A ratio is calculated, weighing factors such as barriers to entry, market risk,

---

[13] Dynamic Parallel Targeting is a registered trademark of SalesForce4Hire, LLC.

adoption rate, and market penetration expense divided by a common denominator of value to the targeted prospect and earnings potential.

Dynamic Parallel Targeting®
Decision Matrix

	Segment A	Segment B	Segment C	Segment D
Total Market Size	$500,000,000	$150,000,000	$300,000,000	$200,000,000
Market Growth (CAGR)*	6%	12%	4%	2%
Barriers To Entry	1	2	4	3
Market Risk	1	2	5	5
Adoption Rate	1	5	2	3
Penetration Expense	3	3	4	3
Numerator	3	12	15	14
Value To Prospect	5	5	4	3
Earnings Potential	5	4	3	2
Common Denominator	10	9	7	5
Risk/Return Ratio	0.6	1.34	2.14	2.8
Segment Ranking	1st	2nd	3rd	4th

*CAGR ~ Current Annual Growth Rate

Dynamic Parallel Targeting is a registered trademark of SalesForce4Hire, LLC.

Not all of the factors considered in the equations are quantifiable beyond experience, supposition, and intuition. The creation of a comparable baseline, however, proved to be invaluable in determining the prioritization of investments in competing market segments. It also provided a structured framework for the leadership team to discuss, explore, and debate the suppositions. This approach can deliver exceptional clarity when bringing a disruptive technology like adult stem cells, to the marketplace, a technology that has never existed before and lacks historical market data.

The values assigned to the various risk and expense points, the sum of which determines the numerator in developing the risk to return ratio, are assigned a value from one to five. The higher the number, the greater the risk or expense associate with the category of consideration. The values assigned to categorize the value to the segment prospect and earnings potential, which determines the *common denominator*, follow the same pattern; the higher the value (of one through five) the higher the number assigned. The resulting ratio enables a side by side comparison to occur, the lowest ratio value reflecting the best risk to return opportunity in the shortest period of time. This is especially helpful in a start-up environment where resources are limited and the organization is burning investor capital prior to generating revenue. More obvious variables such as market size and current annual growth rate speak for themselves and help guide the prioritization process.

Employing Dynamic Parallel Targeting is an excellent way to begin cultivating intuition throughout the organization. Begin by discussing the factors that are used to calculate the numerator with your team. Challenge each other's assumptions throughout the discussion and intentionally come to no conclusions at the time. Ask everyone to sleep on their thoughts and encourage them to reflect on how they feel about their assumptions, openly expressing how you value their intuition. Gather again in the next day or two and revisit the conversation and then conduct the calculation. Alternating between asking how they feel and how they think will also emphasize the value you place on their intuition. It builds trust and elevates the holistic appreciation you have for all of their skills and cultivates their willingness to give more of themselves in the process.

One area where you will probably want to concentrate on hard market research is in the defining of your prospect. You would be surprised how many companies expend resources and energy in the marketplace on misaligned call points.

There are two types of call points most companies will incur, especially if they are marketing a sophisticated, high value product or service. The first is a buying influence. This can be a purchasing agent, a quality assurance professional, or another person that will have some level of input in the decision making process. The other is the actual prospect, or decision maker in their acquisition process.

A prospect can be defined using a process developed by Kevin Schimelfenig called IA^2®[14]. IA^2 qualifies a prospect as someone that has the *intellectual* capacity to embrace your value proposition, the *ability* to afford your product or service, and the *authority* to sign the purchase order. All three attributes must be present to qualify a buying influence as a prospect.

Taking the time to fully understand the difference between your buying influences and true prospects will accelerate your success in the marketplace. A thorough understanding of your prospect's buying criteria will enable you to focus on what it is about your value proposition that is most important to them. If you can align your value with your prospect's objectives you will find yourself communicating effectively and be viewed as an asset, as an ally, rather than simply another company vying for their resources. This is a key to differentiating your company in highly competitive and noisy markets.

---

[14] IA^2 is a registered trademark of SalesForce4Hire, LLC.

~ Assessing Risks and Threats

When assessing threats to your success it is important to view the risk that can emerge from within the organization as well as from outside of the organization. It is helpful to write this out in two separate tables. One should focus on internal threats and related responses, the other detailing threats that exist outside of the company and your possible contingencies to address these factors.

You will find the source of most internal threats outlined in the weaknesses section of your Self-Assessment. This is a good time to think about how you plan to address your weaknesses so they don't derail the realization of your vision. Can you see how the planning process begins to align the enterprise with your vision?

One significant internal threat that is a constant companion to us all is simply this: You don't know what you have yet to experience. There is a learning curve associated with everything we do in life. This learning curve can be especially steep when entering into a market that is new to you. It is also true when you are entering familiar markets with a disruptive technology. A simple definition of a disruptive technology is something that thoroughly challenges dogma by enabling an entirely new approach to existing methodologies.

The curve can be steeper still if you are bringing a disruptive technology into a Blue Ocean market. Blue Ocean markets are markets that you are creating for the very first time with the introduction of your product or service. As such, Blue Ocean markets have no competition and also have no historical reference points for your potential customers. Some familiar examples of Blue Ocean markets were electricity, the telephone, railroads, personal computers, and internet commerce. The opposite of Blue Ocean markets are Red Ocean markets; existing markets in which the only way new customers can be acquired is by taking market share from a competitor, thus spilling blood into the market space.

The point is, the further out on the forefront you are in commercialization there will be things that are inherently unknown until you engage in the process. In these environments it is likely the only illumination you may have along your path is your intuition. Another significant internal risk that warrants considerable attention is the threat that can emerge from a dysfunctional organizational culture.

External threats will come at you from two directions; from competition and from market drivers. Market drivers are the big issues that affect everyone. They can include (but are not limited to) macro-economic factors (i.e. the economic cycle, currency exchange rates, or interest rates), demographic trends, technological evolution, policy issues (i.e. international trade agreements, government regulations), and unforeseen political or social upheaval. What may appear to be a difficult hurdle may in fact be a wonderful opportunity depending upon how you anticipate and position your enterprise to address the factor. Examining the market drivers will help you and your team see things from various sides of a particular issue. Think from the perspective of your company, your competition, and your prospects and you may be surprised by what you see. This is another area where sifting through the market data from differing perspectives can fuel your intuitive insights.

Identifying the competitive landscape can have varying degrees of difficulty. If your competitors are publicly traded companies, you should be able to find substantial information on their annual sales, historical growth rates, and strategic focus. Annual reports, SEC filings, and their corporate websites offer a plethora of information. If you are competing with privately held companies this information is more difficult to come by.

One source of information on private companies is from their customers. By taking the time to develop a dialogue with the customer base, you can begin to gain insights into the strengths and weaknesses of your competitors. Listen to what people laud in their evaluation of the competitor as well as to what they may dislike. This is another area where intuition can come into play. The closer you get to the market and the more engaged you are with customers, insights will begin to emerge. Over time you will develop a feel for where the competition is and where they may be going strategically.

Another great way to gauge the trends in a market is by attending industry trade shows and symposia. Smaller companies are often represented in their trade show booths by their executive teams, marketing professionals, and their best sales representatives. Make note of some key indicators that you can observe by visiting their booth. What is the condition of the booth property? Are they focusing on existing products or introducing new technologies? Are they busy with prospects throughout the day? How excited are their booth visitors? How enthusiastic are the sales people? What's their body language telling you? How are you greeted and treated when you introduce yourself and they realize (if they do) you're a competitor? In other words, try to get the feel for how they are resonating into the marketplace. Be sure to attend any presentations or roundtable discussions they may be conducting. This will give you insight into what they think is important to their strategic direction. Involve your teammates in this process as well and include their perceptions in your evaluation.

~ Key Concepts
- Engaging your intuition can be a powerful tool augmenting your Market Assessment.
- Focus on creating a flourishing, preferential advantage. Focus on your customers!
- Be aware of your competition, but beware obsessing over them.
- Build a Decision Matrix to evaluate and prioritize competing opportunities.
- Address your weaknesses and leverage your core competencies.

~ Exercise

Create a Decision Matrix using Dynamic Parallel Targeting for the various market opportunities in your business. Identify market size, current annual growth rates, barriers to entry, market risk, adoption rates, and penetration expense for each segment to calculate your numerator. Identify your value to your customer and your company's earning potential for each segment to calculate your denominator. Compare and evaluate your priorities.

Chapter Six ~
Clarity and Communication:
Vision and Mission Statements

"In the attitude of silence the soul finds the path in a clearer light, and what is elusive and deceptive resolves itself into crystal clearness." Mahatma Gandhi

We have now embarked upon the strategic planning process with a vision, an inspiration for the journey about to unfold before us. The first steps upon our path took us inward, towards our authentic selves, accessing the ancient and perennial wisdom that resides within us all. From this vantage point we then looked outward, surveying the landscape we are to traverse in the manifestation of our vision. Hopefully this process of reflection, investigation, and contemplation has created a degree of focus, a refined acuity to your original vision. If so, it is time to carefully craft your vision with words of clarity and inspiration, words which reflect your intention, words that will resonate in the hearts and minds of others.

In my experience I have often found this to be one of the most challenging phases of the strategic planning process. Perhaps this is due to its importance. The intention that you will express through the writing of your Vision and Mission Statements will be akin to that first pebble dropped into the stillness of a pool at dawn. The attitude that radiates outward will establish the initial impression everyone will feel when first encountering your company. It is simultaneously the baseline and the zenith of the culture you are about to create. How this resonates will determine who is attracted to your cause. The articulate calibration of the message you are about to generate will require meticulous attention to your intention and the language you choose in its expression.

Let's start with the Mission Statement. It defines your company's raison d'être, its reason for being. It should explain your company's purpose, how you go about fulfilling that purpose, and resonate clearly with your intention and organizational values. It may be helpful to approach the writing of your Mission Statement from two distinct vantage points.

The first approach in creating your Mission Statement is to review the assessment sections of your plan. The Market Assessment should have helped you identify your target market, prospects, and the priorities you have established for pursuing these various segments. Your reason for being in business should strongly correlate to delivering a distinct value proposition with your priority market segments.

Now review your core competencies. Remember the definition? These should be strengths unique to your enterprise that contribute a flourishing preferential advantage to your company in the eyes of your prospects. The manner in which you leverage your core competencies should define how you intend to serve your customers.

The final step in this approach is to examine how you plan to address your weaknesses identified in your Self-Assessment. This will resonate with the core values of the organization. In other words, it will reflect how you value your people and where and how you intend to invest in them to improve the company. No matter the weakness, it most likely will be overcome through the application of human capital in one form or another. Even a lack of financial resources will be addressed by the quality of your management team.

This review of your earlier work should help you find the language that communicates why you're in business, how you do business, and what your values are in the conduct of your business.

The other approach that can be helpful in creating your Mission Statement is soliciting the input of your associates. Try conducting this exercise during a white board session. Gather your associates in a quiet room and write three questions on a white board: First, what is the market need we fulfill? Second, how do we address this need? And finally, what are the guiding principles that guide our business activities? Have your associates write and anonymously submit their answers and transcribe them onto the board for discussion.

This can be an eye opener and it is an especially useful tool for understanding how your culture is evolving. How you perceive the business may be very different from the way your associates perceive the business. This exercise is an excellent way to get a feel for the collective consciousness of the organization and the resulting tenor of the culture.

This process may also reveal underlying disconnects that may exist between different constituencies within the organization. Does your development team perceive the business in the same manner as your sales and marketing team? Does accounting's vision differ from the customer service team's understanding of the mission? Getting everyone on the same page is a major step in creating a powerful, transformational culture. Conducting this type of review is an inexpensive and highly effective way to clarify minor misunderstandings and to bridge the gaps that tend to arise between functional groups within the business.

There is also substantial value in extending this exercise to include your customers, your investors, your partners, and vendors. This can help you determine if you are projecting your intention accurately. The feedback you get will be a genuine reflection of the cultural energy the business is resonating and whether it is the intended outcome or not.

Examining your mission will bring clarity to many issues. It will help management understand the type of associates that are attracted to your company and why some are excelling while others may not be thriving. Are you attracting the level of character you want within your company? Is there a disconnection between management and associates? Is there a disconnection between fellow associates? Are you attracting the type of customers you want? Do you have the right kind of partners and do they share in your vision? This exercise will provide insight as to why you are succeeding or why you are not succeeding and identify areas within your business that may require your leadership and attention.

It may be helpful to review an actual Mission Statement to get a better feel of what you may wish to express. Here's the Mission Statement for my company, Performance Transformation, LLC:

Performance Transformation, LLC aligns and integrates leadership, strategy, and culture through the Accretive Coaching Process™ igniting sustainable, breakthrough performance in a mindful, respectful manner.

It answers the three main questions in succinct language that resonates with the intention of the organization. First, our purpose is to assist human beings and organizations achieve breakthrough performance. Second, the manner in which we do so is by helping organizations develop and align their leadership, strategy and culture. We do so through our Accretive Coaching Process in a way that embraces and respects the human element of business.

Our Mission Statement also infers our intent to create dynamic improvements (note the choice of the verb *igniting*). We're not trying to deliver small, incremental improvements in performance. Our evidence-based research and decades of experience drives the transformational effect our approach delivers in organizations. The passion of our purpose is evident in the language we chose.

The clarity of our message resonates strongly with some people and not as much with others. That's okay; this is our intention. We want to attract associates, partners, and clients that will readily embrace our value proposition. We know we are at the forefront of change and realize we cannot expend energy trying to convince people that will struggle to understand our philosophy. We understand the clients we attract will already be at a certain level of consciousness in order to understand our approach. Our intention is clear and it resonates through our Mission Statement.

Take your time in cultivating your Mission Statement. It will most likely take you more than a few passes to dial in on the right message. Don't let this discourage you; it took our organization several months to find the words that clearly express our mission. Write a draft and walk away from it for a day or two. Engage in your favorite outdoor activity, get some exercise, commune with nature, relax and let the message come to you. Jot down thoughts that come to you regarding the key values you wish to emphasize. Even if they don't fit into the Mission Statement you may wish to establish a list of Value Statements that augment your company's philosophy. Let your intuition guide you as it will be highly aligned with your intention.

Now that you're well into the planning process, it may seem that certain aspects may appear out of logical order. At first glance, you may wonder why we weren't writing the Vision Statement at the time we were initially discussing your Vision, before we began the assessment phase of the process.

You see, each step of the strategic planning process is intended to bring a higher degree of acuity to the creative visualization of your business. It is intended to integrate and unleash the power of your emotional, cognitive, and spiritual intelligence while weaving it into pragmatic, highly effective business practices. As we tap into all of our centers of intelligence that reside within us, the constraints of linear thinking fade away. Our intuition does not require us to go from point A to point B in order to arrive at point C.

By focusing the intention of your Vision through the Self-Assessment, Market Assessment, and Mission Statement process you are hopefully elevating yourself to a higher place of intention that is exponentially more powerful than if we had attempted to write it in the beginning. With your newfound clarity you are ready to write your Vision Statement.

The Vision Statement is a vivid, energetic affirmation of your desired outcome. It should motivate and inspire your associates, your customers, your partners, and your self. The language you choose in the expression of your Vision Statement is of the utmost importance.

Words have enormous energetic power, both spoken, and especially written. A scientist by the name of Dr. Masaru Emoto has demonstrated the energetic power of words by showing the effects words have on crystal formations in water.[15] Dr. Emoto wrote both positively intentioned words (like *love* and *thank you*) and negatively intentioned words (like *ugly* and *hate*) onto paper and

---

[15] I recommend reading the works of Dr. Masaru Emoto. His recent book, "The Miracle of Water", Atria Books, New York, Beyond Words Publishing, Hillsborough, OR, 2007, is a wonderful place to begin exploring his scientific research. Fascinating stuff!

attached them to jars of water. The crystals that formed when freezing the water exposed to positive words created beautiful patterns. The water that had been exposed to negative words created deformed, asymmetrical crystals. Interestingly, it didn't matter what particular language was used, the results were the same!

When you consider we are all energetic vibration (remember the lessons from quantum physics) physically manifested primarily in the form of water (more than 70% of a human being is comprised of water) it makes one wonder. I think we can appreciate the powerful repercussions words may also have on human beings. The words you choose in the expression of your Vision have an energy all their own. Carefully and consciously choosing your words to reflect your intention will create a positive frequency that will emphatically resonate with your constituents.

We have discussed on several occasions how all matter is, at its essence, energy vibrating at a specific frequency. Let's reflect on this a bit more. Dense matter, such as stone, vibrates at a low frequency and can be slow to change, yet it can still erode from the energy of matter vibrating at higher frequencies such as water or air.

Thoughts, and thoughts expressed through language, vibrate at a high frequency and are relatively easy to change. Quantum physics has taught us that we are all connected in the energy field that is the universe. What we interpret as reality, say a tree, is energy defined or calibrated by the frequency of its information. Our awareness is limited by the level of our consciousness enabling us to interpret, through our senses, the energetic frequencies that surround us in our world. The more closely we align the language we choose (our information) with our intentions (our energy) the more powerful and impactful this frequency will be to all who encounter it!

We are all creators in this world. We all have the power to create and influence the reality that unfolds before us. In moments of quiet reflection I have found amazement in the fact that I have been able to create entire businesses out of a single idea through its expression in language. It wasn't until I began to experience my own spiritual awakening that I started to realize how the mechanics of this wondrous process actually work.

I now understand that the strategic planning process is a series of increasingly specific affirmations of creative visualization. With each level of specificity, the affirmations move closer to manifestation until the collective energy of the business team's intention carries the visualization into a reality far exceeding our initial expectations! I have also come to appreciate it is the clear and consistent expression of the Vision Statement that helps anchor this process. The Vision Statement serves as a sort of touchstone all associates can revisit to during challenging moments.

The strategic planning process also empowers the business team to focus in the moment, to be entirely present, because the plan has identified the daily tactics we need to implement to be successful. We need not worry about next month, next quarter, or next year. We trust our shared Vision and we are empowered to remain focused on the tasks before us. The tasks that move us towards success. As a result, the business takes on an energetic life of its own and lifts us all into a wonderfully purposeful and profitable reality! Keeping these thoughts in mind, how each step of the process brings us closer to creating our desired outcome, will help guide the writing of the Vision Statement.

First, be bold! Don't allow your vision to be hemmed in by perceived limitations based upon what exists today.

You're about to create something totally new and you will be well served in maintaining the knowledge you are capable of creating an entirely new way of doing things, an entirely new way of seeing things, an entirely new world! The only limiting factor is you, so don't buy into the nay-sayers. Even if you are working within an existing business, a new vision can transform it entirely.

Remember my story about STERIS Corporation and Bill Sanford? His vision transformed the global standard of care for minimally invasive surgery while the dominant sterilization company of the last century turned a blind eye to the concept. Creative power resides within us all. It is time you express your intention with the strongest of affirmations!

Your Vision Statement should look out into the future at least five years. Yet, to give it power you should express it as if it has already come into being. A dear friend and colleague of mine, Mike Briglia, used to joke with me as we were writing the strategic plan for a new global service business, "As it is written, so it is done." His words proved to ring with a truth neither of us could have completely imagined at the time. Within two years this new business had grown to employ more than 185 professionals operating in twenty countries generating annual revenues of $35 million. Our Vision Statement expressed the goals we hoped to accomplish in five years yet we exceeded our expectations within 24 short months!

Here is the Vision Statement for my company, Performance Transformation, LLC:

Performance Transformation, LLC is the leading provider of transformational services for organizations seeking to cultivate and leverage their human talent. Our approach delivers a flourishing, preferential advantage in rapidly evolving global markets.

Let's examine the construction of this statement. First, the company assumes a leadership position, it does not follow; it innovates. Second, the statement speaks directly to organizations that are seeking substantive change to their current business modality. Companies that are comfortable in their current state are not a target and in fact would perceive the intention of Performance Transformation as disruptive (it is, but in very positive ways). The company is a change agent that delivers transformational benefits to its clientele, but the client must first be seeking change.

They must share a similar philosophy in order to embrace the value offered. The intention is focused on delivering dynamic, new ways of thinking, leading, planning, organizing, and functioning that enable companies to flourish in the highly fluid and evolutionary global environment of today and beyond.

Another phrase that expresses an important aspect of the organization's intention is *flourishing preferential advantage*. This has evolved from the traditional *continuous competitive advantage*. The intention is to shift organizational focus to the customer in order to build an ever increasing preference for the enterprise's products or services. While it makes sense to be aware of what the competition is doing, focusing too much time and energy on them represents a predatory mindset that will inevitably show up in relationship with one's customers. By focusing on the needs and preferences of the customer, a company will build strong relationships that will serve both parties in fair and equitable exchange. This represents a truly differentiating advantage and it emerges through focused intention.

Earlier in the chapter I mentioned Value Statements. These are statements that round out the expression of the organization's intentions and core values. Value Statements often speak of the commitment the company has towards its associates, community, and environment. One of the most powerful Value Statements I've ever encountered was from STERIS Corporation: "No activity, other than safety on the job, is more important than taking care of the Customer."

This may appear fundamental and obvious, but when you consider many associates spend more than fifty percent of their time on activities that do not contribute directly to the satisfaction of their customers it may be worth serious consideration. Note that *Customer* is a proper noun in the statement. This reflected the intention of being *customer-centric*, of building all of our processes and activities around the needs of our customers. Value Statements such as this can prove to be a touchstone to the organization in times of crisis or uncertainty and can serve as the supporting tenets of organizational culture.

Such statements can serve to empower associates, especially as the organization grows in size and the pace of daily market activities escalates. Early in my executive career at STERIS a field manager came to me requesting guidance in making a decision regarding the expenditure of company resources in support of a customer request. I asked the manager if he felt it was the right thing to do. He responded that he thought it was and it would build goodwill with a potentially strategic customer. I then instructed him that he need not ask me for permission, he need only ask himself if he would be comfortable defending his decision with the CEO. If he felt comfortable answering for his decision because it was aligned with our company values then he should go ahead and do it.

He need not ask permission, it was already granted through the clear articulation of our values. Our associates were empowered to act upon the benefit of our customers in a clear and timely manner.

As a leader, you should communicate these statements at every opportunity. Have them printed and display them clearly in each work area (at STERIS miniature copies were printed and laminated so we could carry them in our wallets). Open every formal meeting or presentation with the articulation of these values. Engrain them like a mantra into the shared consciousness of your associates. Never forget, "As it is written, so it is done"!

~ Key Concepts

- Your Mission Statement expresses your reason for being in business.
- Your Vision Statement is your keystone affirmation.
- The clarity of your intention calibrates your shared consciousness.
- The expression of your values sustains your organizational culture.

~ Exercise

Solicit input from your closest friends, family members, and confidants regarding their impression of your Vision. Ask them to answer the following questions:

- What is the market need my business serves?
- How does the business intend to address this need?
- What is your impression of my guiding business principles?

Reflect on their answers. How well have you articulated your vision to the people closest to you? This will provide insight into the clarity of your Vision, Mission, and values.

Chapter Seven ~
Articulation of Affirmations:
Goals, Objectives, Strategies, and Tactics

"Planning is bringing the future into the present so that you can do something about it now" Alan Lakein

Strategic planning is the articulation of increasingly specific affirmations of creative visualization. The execution of your plan will draw the collective consciousness of your entire business team together in a creative orchestration of movement and resonance towards the manifestation of your Vision. The disciplined, daily focus it delivers empowers the entire enterprise to function in the present moment, to focus its collective energy in the now. It is a remarkable actualization to be a part of and an exhilarating process to lead. You will find that the combination of group intention, collective consciousness, and presence unleashes an energy that is far greater than the sum of its parts.

You started this process with a Vision of where you wish to go on your journey. From there you assessed your self and the current position of the company. From the perspective of knowing where you are and knowing where you wish to go, you then surveyed the landscape you must navigate in order to find your path. With the knowledge of the market assessment in hand, you then formally expressed your intention, purpose, values, and Vision through the articulation of your first, formal affirmations. The fundamentals are now in place to begin the actual strategic planning phase of the process. This will serve as your action plan.

Each step of the strategic planning process moves you from creative visualization in the abstract sense towards manifestation in the absolute sense. To paraphrase Thoreau, you have built your castle in the air with your Vision, it is now time to build the foundation beneath it!

The first step is the articulation of your Goals. I like to describe Goals as "what I want to be when I grow up" statements. Your Goals should be grand and sweeping affirmations of what you wish to achieve three to five years down the road written in the present tense in order to ignite the statements with creative energy.

Your Goals are realized through the actualization of your Objectives. Objectives are measurable gates set within a certain timeframe, usually the current operating year, and are achieved through the execution of your Strategies. Strategies are the initiatives that position your company, determine value propositions, pricing, marketing communications, and operating procedures. Finally, Tactics are the day-to-day activities, the focus on doing and being in the present, that, when engaged, implement your Strategies. It is through the articulation and execution of this process that your foundation is set and the pillars of achievement are initiated.

For clarification let's use a soccer analogy as an example of the process. It is the beginning of the second half of a game tied at zero to zero. You know you must score a Goal in order to win the game. You set an Objective of pressing the play in the opponent's end for the majority of the second half. You can measure this in terms of the amount of time the ball is in their zone.

Strategically, you decide to bring your mid-fielders further up the field and position them to cut off the passing lanes of the opponent. Subsequently, you also bring your defense forward, knowing that there is a measure of risk here, but one you are willing to incur in order to score a Goal. Tactically, you will depend upon each player to be entirely present in the game, focused on their responsibilities and without the distraction of worrying about what might happen if they lose.

You then coach them to believe in the plan for the second half and the Vision of victory! You have prepared them for this level of play through their training, the practices you have conducted, and their physical conditioning. You have also invested in the appropriate level of talent necessary to carry the day.[16] Your intention is one of confidence, of winning built upon thoughtful and careful preparation for this very moment. Is there any doubt you will score this Goal?

~ Goals

When establishing your Goals it is important to stay concise and closely aligned with your Vision. I know this may sound like a strange source of information, but the U.S. Marine Corps has done extensive studies on how many tasks a soldier can manage while functioning under severe stress. They determined that no more than three objectives should be handled simultaneously by a soldier in

---

[16] Please note that your strategies are only as good as the talent you have placed upon the field and the discipline you have instilled in their dedication and focus on team play! We will explore this further in the next chapter.

the field. Anything beyond this and the individual's performance will diminish dramatically. With this in mind, I have always articulated three Goals, each supported by three Objectives. Strategies and Tactics fan out in greater number as the responsibility for them will be delegated throughout the organization.

In fact, I usually only express two unique Goals in the planning process, reserving one for a perennial Goal I traditionally expressed when creating a strategic plan; *Ensure Customer Satisfaction.* To me this is paramount no matter the vision, fore without satisfied customers you will not be in business for long. This also serves organizationally as the place where I establish the operational objectives such as the establishment of support infrastructure that are mission critical to efficient functionality and success.

I recently came across some research published by a major, multi-national consulting firm that has caused me to rethink and re-articulate this Goal statement. Their research emerged through the prism of Applied Behavioral Economics (the integration of economic theory with psychology). The study indicates that rationally satisfied customers are no more likely to purchase more or continue their relationship with a vendor than dissatisfied customers. Wow! There's an eye-opener! The research goes on to state that the difference comes through engaging the customer on an emotional level. The customer that feels an emotional connection with a vendor will spend more money and stay with the vendor for years to come.

The researchers actually point to the importance of customers having "passion" for the company, product, or service. (Where have we seen this discussed before?) Apple® is a great example. People that work on a Mac, use an iPhone, an iPad, or an iPod have a passionate loyalty for Apple's products and services. Behavioral economists are shaking up the old, neo-classical economic dogma with substantiated research that now indicates economic decisions may in fact be 70% emotionally driven and 30% rationally driven.

In light of these recent revelations, I've changed the language and intention of my perennial Goal Statement to now read, *Ensure Customer Engagement*. Satisfaction is not enough, success in business requires authentic connection with our customers. This actually aligns more readily with the philosophies we've already explored.

How our customers feel about us is, in fact, as important and perhaps more important than what they think about us!

Goals are expressed as clear affirmations and close derivatives of your Vision Statement. You may be focused on creating breakthrough innovations, exemplary services, or resource conserving solutions to your market. Whatever you envision your company doing from a market leadership position should resonate with your Goals. Think in terms of being the best at what you set out to be. No one sets out to be mediocre, so don't be afraid to stretch your business with aspirational and inspirational Goals!

Stretch Goals are fundamentally critical for the organization. Most people are unaware of how capable they are of growing and ascending to new heights of cognitive performance, emotional intelligence, spiritual awareness, and creative contribution. For a variety of reasons, people are often stuck in a limiting perception of their current condition. The behavioral economists call this *reference dependence*. People perceive possible outcomes from a perspective of how easy it is for them to imagine the outcomes. This is based upon prior experience. By unlocking this prison of perception, an enlightened leader can inspire and motivate remarkable contributions through the continuous growth of their associates.

This isn't an approach of pushing people beyond their comfort zones, as this will only cause entrenchment in most situations. It is a philosophy of pulling people up by directing a bit of air under their wings and reassuring them they can actually soar to new heights. It involves more than simply setting the bar higher, and we will discuss this in detail in the next chapter as we explore talent management, empathy, and building trust.

Stating your Goals is a defining moment for your company. It expresses how you see your enterprise which will resonate with your customers and help create their perceptions of you. In an existing company, Goals can help redefine the entire intention and philosophy of the enterprise. Redefining your Goals can ignite the shift in behavior throughout the organization by kindling a new interpretation of the desired collective consciousness of the company.

Allow me to share an experience I've had in redirecting a company's direction by redefining their Goals. During my corporate career, I was hired by a life science company to provide the strategic and executive leadership necessary to raise annual revenues from $80 million to $250 million in three to five years. The company was an established capital equipment manufacturer with strong brand equity serving the research laboratory marketplace. It was, however, operating in a mature segment and was experiencing sagging sales growth.

The enterprise was on its third owner in less than a decade and throughout all the changes it had developed a convoluted and weak organizational culture that was dominated by fear. Everyone was dug into their organizational foxhole, afraid to lift their heads out from cover in fear of getting them lopped off by the managerial flavor of the week. Two dangerous elements had emerged; first, they defined themselves as an equipment manufacturer and second, they had become inwardly focused on their procurement and manufacturing expertise as their defining core competencies. How they saw themselves limited their ability to innovate, grow, and inspire their associates, channel partners, and customers. The limitations of their own vision had become a self-fulfilling prophecy.

In creating the company's new strategic plan it was critical to redefine the company in an entirely new and dynamic manner. Rather than continue to view ourselves as an equipment manufacturer, we redefined our self image with our first Goal, *Be the Global Leader in Sample Management Solutions*. Our products touched our customers' biological samples at highly critical phases throughout their research. Our products had a direct impact on the quality of our customers' most critical research objectives, yet we had traditionally viewed ourselves in terms that separated us from their lab procedures. By expanding our perspective of how what we did touched the flow of our customers' samples throughout their research we redefined our intention.

We no longer simply manufactured equipment; we now intended to provide solutions to our customers' critical sample management requirements. This expanded vision enabled us to explore new business paradigms of growth through internal development as well as through the acquisition of existing businesses that expanded the role of our involvement with our customers' research. The acquisitions that followed aligned strongly with our core competencies (Manufacturing, Strategic Sourcing, and National Distributor Relationship Management) and enabled us to leverage the economies of scale and distribution that we enjoyed in the marketplace.

This resulted in creating a flourishing preferential advantage that our customers embraced, rapidly distancing our company from our traditional competitors. Rather than attempt to implement small, incremental improvements we had changed the nature of the game and taken a great leap forward in the marketplace!

The second Goal focused directly on the culture, *Express a Customer Focused Business Culture*. This vision enabled us to re-establish our service business into a value-add, lead role within the enterprise. It also enabled us to lift our collective heads out of the trenches to see what our customers needed in support of their endeavors. Again, this was a dramatic change in intention. It empowered us to look outside of our company for innovations that were critical to our customers. This was something we could not have considered prior to the shift in mindset.

This led to creating partnerships and joint ventures with highly innovated, forward thinking entrepreneurs operating at the forefront of the marketplace. This also enabled us to view our channel partners as true customers, thus improving our performance in mission critical ways that contributed to their success and profitability. Of course, the third Goal was, *Ensure Customer Satisfaction* which again shifted the inward looking historical perspective outward towards the marketplace and our customers.

The net effect of this seismic change was nothing short of remarkable. Within thirteen months the company's revenues grew from approximately $80 million per year to more than $300 million per year. Prior to establishing the new strategic direction the company had a market value of approximately $120 million. Four years later, while still maintaining the original vision and direction of the new strategy, the company was sold to a major conglomerate for $750 million dollars. Obviously there was a lot of execution involved in this transformation, but it all began by redefining the internal view of the company through the establishment of a new vision and by refreshing the intention of the enterprise.

~ Objectives

Objectives are relatively easy to identify and define. They are tangible, measurable performance gates within a set time frame, usually within the immediate planning year. I recommend drilling down to some specifics here. Don't settle for, "Grow the business 20% in the current fiscal year." Take the time to identify the specific product or service you intend to grow and in what particular market segment you are targeting for performance. This will help you when you articulate your strategies which, upon implementation, will enable you to achieve your Objectives. In effect, your Objectives are tangible affirmations that, upon manifestation, will bring you one step closer to the realization of your Goals and your Vision.

The key to articulating realistic Objectives capable of moving the business towards the manifestation of your Vision is to ensure you are aligning this process with a sound understanding and acceptance of how things truly are today. This is where enlightened leadership must be just that, enlightened, truly present in the moment, aware and accepting of the strengths, weaknesses, opportunities, and threats to the enterprise. This is also where leadership has the opportunity to send a clear message to the team.

By accepting things as they are and then articulating a clear path forward based upon actionable items, leadership sets a tone of presence for the entire organization. In effect, you are saying we will not expend energy complaining about things or wringing our hands over what we cannot affect in the present. We will focus our collective energy and intention on achieving our Objectives based upon the cards we have been dealt. We understand our constraints and have made plans that will optimize our opportunities based upon our core competencies. We will do what we do best, address what we do not do so well, and work together to move the business forward.

Objectives need not only focus on financial performance criteria. At certain times in the business life-cycle it may be appropriate to set a Goal and supporting Objectives aimed at addressing a strategic weakness of the enterprise. This is especially common in early stage companies. You may have a service or product that will get you into a market but you need to follow up with a second generation of value creation in order to secure long-term success.

Let's go back to the life science company to explore the process in more detail. (Please note, this strategic plan is no longer subject to confidentiality agreements and specific names of people and companies have been removed for privacy considerations). During our Self-Assessment we identified our Strengths, Weaknesses, and Core Competencies (please see following page). In doing so, we identified the differentiating position we held in the marketplace as well as where we needed to focus to

SELF-ASSESSMENT

STRENGTHS	WEAKNESSES
Global Brand Recognition (High Brand Equity)	Low End-User Customer Intimacy
Global Market Share Leader in Core Technology	Historically Reactive Marketing
Market Leading Installed Base	Poor New Product and New Service Pipeline
Rapidly Emerging Sales & Marketing Capabilities	Limited Historical Sales & Marketing Data
Motivated & Focused Leadership Team	Fragmented & Highly Variable Field Service
Well Disciplined & Productive Labor Force	Opportunistic Exporter
Well Respected Technical Support (Call Center)	Inwardly Focused Organizational Culture

CORE COMPETENCIES
✓ Manufacturing Productivity
✓ Strategic Sourcing of Materials
✓ National Distributor Relationship Management

improve our competitive positioning. Remember, to get to where we want to go tomorrow we must first know where we are today. It is from this perspective that we look out into the market landscape in order to assess our opportunities.

In exploring our Market Assessment, we identified our competitive landscape by identifying the companies in which there was some overlap in products, services, and market focus. We identified thirteen companies and assessed them in terms of:

- **Competing Company**
- **Their Market Focus**
- **Their Estimated Annual Revenue**

- **Their Market Differentiation (Strategic Positioning)**
- **Their Strategic Direction**

Through this process we identified not only the threats to our success but our opportunities as well. Today's competitor is often tomorrow's partner. This activity enabled us to identify a future acquisition candidate. When we purchased this company a few months later it more than tripled our size overnight, placing us in a dominant market position within our segment.

The Market Assessment also went on to explore the major market drivers and their implications to our strategy. Market drivers are the tides that lift all boats...macro issues that affect everyone in the marketplace.

This process allowed us to reflect on the current and emerging setting. We could see we were in a healthy, growing market, worthy of capital investment. We also were able to see how the innovation of the sciences (the pending explosion in sample populations, economic value, and growing significance of sample data) were about to collide with the scientist shortage. All this would happen under increasingly rigid quality requirements in the research lab. This emerging confluence of drivers spelled

MARKET DRIVERS	IMPLICATIONS
DEMOGRAPHICS ✓ Rapidly Aging Population ✓ Increasing Longevity	**GROWING DEMAND FOR PHARMACEUTICALS** ✓ Continued Biopharmaceutical Development Demand for Core Products and Services.
GLOBAL COMPETITIVE LANDSCAPE ✓ Scientist Shortage ✓ Intense Drug Development Pipeline Pressures	**ESCALATING PRODUCTION & QUALITY DEMANDS** ✓ Unprecedented Escalation of Productivity Concerns ✓ Migration of Production Quality Assurance Standards into Research Laboratories ✓ Demand for Products & Services Which Optimize Quality Assurance and Research Productivity
TECHNOLOGY ✓ Human Genome Project ✓ Emergence of Stem Cell Research ✓ Improvements in IT	**EMERGENCE OF BIOINFORMATICS & AUTOMATION** ✓ Explosion in Research Sample Populations ✓ Escalation in Research Sample Values ✓ Emerging Demand for Integration of Information Technology with High Volume Sample Process Management Capabilities.
GOVERNMENT POLICIES ✓ Grant Funding Policies (National Institutes of Health) ✓ Rapid Growth in Research Targets/Opportunities	**PRIVATIZATION OF RESEARCH FUNDING** ✓ Growing Influence of Major Pharma in Research Institutes ✓ Migration of Commercial Quality Standards into Traditionally Nonprofit Research Environments ✓ Growing Demand for Services Which Support Migrating Quality Standards & Expectations into Research Markets

one thing...opportunity! The supplier that could help researchers address these challenges could leap ahead of slower to respond competitors. There's nothing more rewarding, in every aspect of that word, than solving problems for customers.

At this point in our strategic journey we were able to discern:

1.) What we did well, what we didn't do well.

2.) What competing companies did and didn't do well. and

3.) What the marketplace was going to need to achieve its own rapidly emerging objectives.

As you can see, it is a fairly simple process when you break it into its various components.

As the executive in charge of strategy in the company, I let this information simmer for a bit, reflecting on the key question: What is the strategic imperative here? My conclusion, one I felt as strongly as I thought, was speed. If I could see what was about to occur I had to assume my competitors did as well.

There was no time to waste. We had to act quickly to address our weaknesses, leverage our strengths and core competencies, and position ourselves as the obvious choice for our customers. This lead to the the final step in the assessment process; Opportunities and Threats (Risks):

OPPORTUNITIES & INITIATIVES	RISKS & RESPONSES
STRATEGIC ADVANTAGE OF RAPIDLY EMERGING SAMPLE REPOSITORIES ✓ Establish Key Accounts & Field Service Strategy ✓ Identify Potential Acquisition Targets	CORE PRODUCT SLIDE TO COMMODITY STATUS ✓ Bundle High, Value-Add Services with Systems Delivering Sample Process Management Solutions to Customers
CUSTOM EQUIPMENT BUSINESS ✓ Establish Sales Targets, Formal Project Management, & Engineering Support Structure	EMERGING REPOSITORY BUSINESS MODEL ✓ Rapidly Enter Business Via Joint Ventures & Acquisitions
ESTABLISH HIGH VALUE-ADD SERVICE PORTFOLIO ✓ Invest in Service Infrastructure ✓ Target Regional Service Companies for Acquisition	EMERGING MICRO/NANO SAMPLING TECHNOLOGY ✓ Develop Capabilities in Core Technology
ESTABLISH PRESENCE IN LABORATORY AUTOMATION MARKETPLACE ✓ Identify Joint Venture Opportunities with Technology Innovators in Laboratory Automation	RAPIDLY EMERGING LABORATORY AUTOMATION TECHNOLOGIES ✓ Commit to Lead Position Via Joint Ventures and Potential Strategic Acquisitions
e-BUSINESS ✓ Invest in Service Business Online Interface	RAPIDLY EMERGING e-BUSINESS DYNAMICS ✓ Leapfrog Competition's e-Commerce Initiatives with e-Service Model
CLARIFY MULTI-NATIONAL STRATEGIC DIRECTION ✓ Migrate to Direct Country Dealer Operations from Regional, Master Dealer Relationships	LOW COST FOREIGN ENTRANTS TO DOMESTIC MARKET ✓ Bundle High, Value-Add Services with Systems Delivering Sample Process Management Solutions to Customers
ESTABLISH CUSTOMER-DRIVEN R&D PROCESS ✓ Introduce Formal Marketing Procedures & Increase Customer Involvement in Innovation & Development	CONTINUED CONSOLIDATION OF MAJOR DISTRIBUTORS ✓ Target Key Accounts with Direct Sales Resources
IMPROVE BRAND & CHANNEL MANAGEMENT ✓ Introduce Formal Marketing Procedures	EROSION OF NATIONAL DISTRIBUTOR SALES SKILL SETS ✓ Target Key Accounts with Direct Sales Resources

With our assessment complete, we knew where we were, where the market was going, where our competition was positioned, where our competition was most likely heading. Most importantly, we had a vision of where we wanted to go and what we needed to do to get there. We were now ready to address *how* we were going to execute. This is what our Goals and Objectives looked like:

BE THE GLOBAL LEADER IN SAMPLE MANAGEMENT SOLUTIONS

✓ Establish a Beachhead in the Sample Repository Business in Current Fiscal Year.

✓ Grow Custom Business Revenue a Minimum of 50% in Current Fiscal Year.

✓ Grow Sample Management & Accessories Revenue a Minimum of 30% in Current Year.

DEVELOP A CUSTOMER FOCUSED BUSINESS CULTURE

✓ Establish a Minimum of $1.5 Million in Field Service Revenue in Current Fiscal Year.

✓ Establish a Functional *e*-Business Interface for Parts & Service in Current Fiscal Year.

✓ Grow Key Accounts Business a Minimum of 30% in Current Fiscal Year.

ENSURE CUSTOMER SATISFACTION

(today I would say Ensure Customer Engagement)

✓ Establish Dealer and Customer Advisory Boards in Current Fiscal Year.

✓ Launch a Minimum of Four New Products & Services Contributing to Customer Quality Assurance in Current Fiscal Year.

✓ Reduce the Cost of Quality a Minimum of 30% in Current Fiscal Year.

The first Goal statement and supporting Objectives directly addressed our need to reinvent how we saw ourselves in the marketplace and aligned us more closely to our customers. The second Goal statement and Objectives addressed our need to change the culture of the organization, again, by more closely aligning ourselves with the needs of our customers through the delivery of services. The third Goal and set of Objectives expressed the importance of the customer and helped us maintain focus on the overriding intention of taking care of the emerging needs of the customer. The Cost of Quality Objective directly addressed quality assurance improvements in protecting the value of our customers' samples within our technology.

With each successive articulation, from Goals to Objectives, and as we'll see, from Strategies to Tactics, the affirmations of creative visualization gain traction throughout the organization. The *action items* become more detailed, disassembling complex processes into manageable tasks. In effect, they become more realistic and conceptually attainable. In doing so, it becomes easier for associates to embrace the Vision, to see how everything will unfold in a natural progression through the execution of daily Tactics.

~ Strategies

Strategies lie at the heart of the planning process. The strategies you choose, and the efficiency of implementation, will have a significant impact upon your journey. It is not surprising that this is also one of the most challenging facets of strategic planning. Strategies are your Your strategies must place you in motion, aligning your value with the customers' endeavors.

Your strategies will directly influence your customers' perceptions of the direction and intention of your commercial processes. How you position your company, how you go to market (distribution and channels), how you communicate (promotion), and how you price your products and/or services will all emerge through your strategies. As they are at the heart of your planning, they should emerge from the perspective of your customers (note the correlation of intention here; keeping your customers at the heart of your endeavors).

The most effective strategies contribute directly to your customers' objectives. Whether you are in a business-to-business (B-to-B) or business-to-consumer (B-to-C) market, you should realize your customers do not engage with your business on your terms. They have their own aspirations, constraints, and objectives that emerge independently from your desires. Your speed to traction will depend, in great part, on how closely you align your intention with the objectives of your customers. Success at aligning interest creates the most effective sales team you will ever have - customers as advocates for your company!

A great place to start in the creation of your strategies is to understand how your company delivers value to your target customers. Does your value proposition contribute directly to the endeavors of your customer? In a B-to-B environment, does it accelerate the attainment of your customers' objectives? Does it save them money or improve directly on their core processes? In a B-to-C environment does your value contribute to your customers' quality of life or satisfy an emotional desire? Understanding these elements will provide insights into how you will need to strategically position your company in the marketplace. It will also help you quantify your pricing strategy, choose your distribution channels, and assist in making wise marketing investments.

The most effective way to cultivate insights into your customers is to get as close as possible to them. Organizations that develop customer intimacy understand both the cause and effects of their target customers' buying decisions.

Many companies use focus groups to try to cultivate these insights. Conventional wisdom considers focus groups to be an efficient and rapid methodology for garnering customer feedback. I've been involved in dozens of focus groups throughout my career and no longer choose to use this method.

On multiple occasions I've observed a peculiar dynamic emerging within focus groups that I believe skews the results of your feedback. I often see a few strong-willed individuals begin to dominate the discourse in an attempt to sway the other participants' opinions. Just human nature, I suppose. It is an artificial environment, one that doesn't exist in the natural marketplace, and the egos and personalities of the participants can deliver a perspective that doesn't necessarily reflect the reality of the buying decision process.

Keep in mind, focus groups are not advisory boards, which should be populated by the opinion leaders or highly influential people in your market that have a long-term interest in your success. If you want to know how and why your customers buy what they do, visit them in the natural surroundings. The environment where your product or service is to be consumed. There are no shortcuts here, but the time you invest will return valuable insights into the reality of your target customers' buying decisions.

By taking a customer-centric approach to developing your strategies you will also gain insights into how your prospects perceive your competition. This is valuable in determining how you choose to position your enterprise.

This is especially critical when entering a market dominated by large competitors, a process that can appear daunting on the surface. Going up against large, well established competition can sometimes be a plus and shouldn't dissuade you from your Vision. Dominant companies can grow complacent or slowly drift away from the realities of their customer base. Bureaucratic, high-priced, insulated leadership, and the sheer weight of a large organization can slowly become self involved and internally focused, losing sight of what it was that propelled them into a dominant position in the first place.

By developing authentic relationships with your prospects, and showing a sincere interest in their objectives, you will open a revealing and honest discourse. Areas of dissatisfaction, unmet needs, or new opportunities to deliver value will appear. Sometimes just by doing the smallest of things in a slightly different manner will differentiate you from the competition in very meaningful ways to your customers. Take the time to really listen and your prospects will tell you everything they want from the relationship. This will reveal the strategic positioning you should pursue.

I learned these lessons first hand as a young salesman working for a tiny distributor in the life science market back in the 1980's. The company was located in

Massachusetts and only had nine employees. I was one of two sales representatives with the company. My territory was Cambridge, which, along with San Francisco, was a hotbed of the emerging biotechnology industry at the time. We had many of the exact same products as Baxter Scientific Products, Fisher Scientific, Curtin Matheson, and VWR, all very large, national distributors targeting the same market. The company I worked for did, however, choose to private label many of these products. This, in combination with my ability to focus on a relatively small geography, created a perception with my customers that we were a major player in the marketplace just like the large distributors.

As I grew to understand the cultures of my customers' organizations I began to reposition myself vis-à-vis my competition. I was calling on M.I.T., Harvard, and the tiny, entrepreneurial companies that were continuously popping up all around Cambridge. What are now some of the largest and most profitable biotechnology companies in the world were, at the time, working out of tiny laboratories located along the cobblestoned, back side streets.

I came to appreciate the level of altruism the laboratory scientists expressed through their career choice. These were some of the brightest, most talented human beings I would ever come to know, and in the 1980's there was very little money to be made pursuing a career path in research. By simply letting my customers know we were a small, local company, the David versus Goliaths of the industry, I repositioned myself in their eyes. I was a little guy, just like them, doing my small part in fighting the good fight.

I didn't represent Corporate America and this greatly appealed to their sensibilities. This, combined with taking the time to understand the challenges they faced in their research, enabled me to eventually be viewed as a resource rather than a salesman. This resulted in my achieving unprecedented access to key researchers throughout the community and the tripling of my territory's sales revenue.

The insights gained through understanding the challenges of your target prospects also helps develop a fair and accurate pricing strategy. Many companies, especially early stage entrepreneurial companies, tend to lean towards a "me-too" or a cost-plus pricing strategy. Young companies will look to the market leader and price themselves accordingly, often with a discount mentality. Even worse is looking at one's cost and then deciding on a margin of comfort. Either approach ignores the true value proposition you are offering your customers and are, in effect, internally focused strategies.

Your customers are not concerned with your costs and looking solely at your competition ignores a customer-centric philosophy of value creation. The advanced wound care company discussed earlier in the book is a good example. Until we came to understand the magnitude of the clinical problem we could not intelligently price the technology. The manufacturing cost had nothing to do with the value proposition we were about to offer the clinicians, hospital administrators, patients, and eventually the federal government, insurance companies, employers, and society at large.

The competing products offered by the big multi-nationals also had nothing to do with the creative approach we had discerned for our strategic positioning. Our positioning staked a leadership claim to a new and innovative approach to a problem the competition had failed to fully resolve. The strategy chose to lead with an intention of altruism and a Vision of what is possible versus what is impossible.

In developing our go-to-market strategy, we consciously chose to lead the way to a new horizon rather than following the well worn path of marginal clinical efficacy and value. In doing so we were able to identify pricing that accurately reflected our value to our customers while still being fair and reasonable.

Your positioning strategy will also set your direction for long-term growth and the dissemination of your business throughout the broader market landscape. The positioning strategy we developed for the wound care company first sought to take on one of the most challenging segments of the health care delivery system. By providing a clinically efficacious and affordable therapy that could help avoid amputations, the company would lead with its intention. In doing so, it would lay the foundation for reimbursement and open the door for growth into the much larger decubitus ulcer (bedsore) market segment in long-term care environments.

To get an idea of how significant this clinical problem is we need only look to the tragic tale of actor Christopher Reeves. Even with the finest health care available that enabled Mr. Reeves to survive a crippling horse fall that left him paralyzed, it was a bedsore that took his life. Bedsores are one of the greatest challenges effecting nursing homes and require substantial clinical attention and expensive therapies.

The positioning strategy of solving a crisis in personal suffering within financially stressed inner-city hospitals would propel the therapy to standard of care status in this relatively small, yet clinically critical setting. This would lead to reimbursement coding, and a broader adoption into another therapeutic application. By closely intertwining your strategies with the unmet needs of your customers, your company will engage the marketplace. This builds momentum that will help carry you towards the realization of your Vision.

Your positioning strategy will also clarify your marketing strategy. Understanding how you are positioned with your customers will enable you to define your communications needs as well as the tone of your message. One thing you should keep in mind. While their aspirations and concerns are often quite similar, people of different professions, cultures, and educational backgrounds assimilate, process, and embrace information differently. We live in a world crowded with marketing. We are quite literally bombarded by thousands of commercial messages a day. The closer you are to your customer base the more articulate you will be in your message. The closer you are to your intention, the greater your message will resonate with your customers.

~ Tactics

Tactics are the most immediate of your affirmations. They are the day-to-day activities that implement your Strategies. Tactics enable your associates to focus in the moment, to stay on task without worrying about the past or the future. This focus in the present contributes to the cumulative energy of your organization's collective consciousness. Getting everyone on the same page, moving in the same direction, at the same time, creates remarkable momentum for the enterprise.

This is where the collective intention of a well orchestrated company resonates beyond the sum of its individual parts. I've experienced this numerable times first-hand. On countless occasions, well before we had implemented fifty to sixty percent of our strategies, we would find ourselves tracking to one hundred percent of our objectives! This phenomenon mystified me for years until I realized it was the cumulative, creative energy of the team that was making our Vision a reality. Everyone was expressing an authentic, shared intention delivering powerful actions in the daily focus of our business.

Tactics are also a useful tool for guiding day-to-day, conscious leadership. Tactics enable leadership to delegate responsibilities with clarity, eliminating ambiguity throughout the organization. Ambiguity of peoples' roles, responsibilities, and areas of authority is the seed of discontent and anxiety in an enterprise. When people are unsure of their situation, of where they stand on the team, they quickly exit the present and begin to worry about the future. Nothing derails productivity faster than a team looking ahead of their tasks-at-hand, consumed with the worry of self-preservation.

It is a natural response based upon what they have learned through past experiences from working in unconscious organizations. It cultivates a freeze, fight or flight mentality and replaces the *we* with *me*. By clearly articulating everyone's place and value in delivering upon the Vision through the use of concise Tactics, many of these fears can be avoided.

The management of Tactics is best delineated through the use of a process called Management by Objectives. Delegating a reasonable number of tactical responsibilities on a quarterly basis, in writing, throughout the team, will enable leadership to create a measurement standard for the progress of the strategic plan's implementation. It also provides a communication tool for assigning areas of responsibility that are process focused rather than territorially focused. This can be used for providing performance feedback on a continuous basis and is a fair and understood baseline for performance based incentives. This approach helps keep people focused on the actionable tasks supporting the Vision on a daily basis. Team members know what is expected of them, understand their role in the mission in relation with each other, and have a working guideline to keep them focused in the present moment.

The tactical distribution of tasks in written form is an invaluable tool for rapidly growing businesses. It enables leadership to quickly assess where they are, what is working, and what may require additional attention or resources. By reviewing their team's management objectives followed by simply touching base with their associates' daily progress, a conscious leader can assess the focus of the organization. This will also identify behaviors that may be creating friction within the culture. Three very simple questions can be asked on a daily basis that can contribute to a company's momentum:

- Are we following the intention of our plan or are we drifting off task?
- If we are drifting off task, why?

and

- Are our current activities focused on delivering value to our customers?

Having a thoughtfully expressed and clearly communicated strategic plan is an actionable tool for guiding execution.

~ A Living Document

Your strategic plan is not meant to be an infallible tomb of wisdom collecting dust on the shelf. It is a living document the entire organization employs on a daily basis. Each time it is reviewed by members of your organization it reinforces the intention of your Vision. As you engage your marketplace you will come upon new opportunities that will naturally arise along your path. These may require a calibration of your plan.

Interestingly, I've found that by having a well disciplined plan unanticipated, profitable opportunities tend to reveal themselves with greater frequency. This is perhaps due to the fact that awareness and engagement tend to be higher when following this disciplined approach. Remember, we don't know what we have yet to experience, and going to market will definitely be an experience!

Refer to your plan frequently and be prepared to move in response to your opportunities. Ensure everyone has a copy of the plan that needs to have one (certain members of your team may require the entire document, but you may choose to distribute detailed segments in a judicious manner to help team members stay focused on their particular Tactics and Strategies).

On the following page is a format for strategic planning that I have used more than forty times and it has always served me well. Let's reference the life science company once again. On a single sheet of paper you can review your Goals, Objectives, Strategies, and Tactics as well as begin to budget for execution.

The consistent use of this approach has resulted in more than $1 billion in market valuation growth through my career. Not to be confused with revenue growth, market valuation is the value of the company if it were to be sold (more than two thirds of this figure was actually realized

GOAL ~ BE THE GLOBAL LEADER IN SAMPLE MANAGEMENT SOLUTIONS

OBJECTIVE #1 ~ Establish a Beachhead in Sample Repository Business in Current Fiscal Year

STRATEGY #1 ~ Acquire Core Technologies Necessary to Accelerate Business Launch

TACTIC	RESPONSIBILITY	TIME FRAME	ADD TO STAFF	COST	PROJECTED REVENUE	GROSS MARGIN%
Acquire "A" Company	Assign Staff	Q1	35	In Negotiation	$6 Million	>45%
Acquire Archive Technology Platform from "B" Company	Assign Staff	Q1	5	In Negotiation	$800,000	>50%
Evaluate Joint Venture with "C" Company in Order to Acquire Marketing Rights and Ownership Option for Laboratory Automation Technology	Assign Staff	Q1	n/a	In Negotiation	TBD	TBD

STRATEGY #2 ~ Establish Sample Repository in the Northeast Corridor

TACTIC	RESPONSIBILITY	TIME FRAME	ADD TO STAFF	COST	PROJECTED REVENUE	GROSS MARGIN%
Establish Formal Strategic Alliance with "D" Corporation	Assign Staff	Q1	-	-	-	-
Identify & Lease Operating Facility	Assign Staff	Q1	-	$100,000	-	-
Hire & Train Facility Staff	Assign Staff	Q2	2	$130,000	-	-
Establish & Implement Standard Operating Procedures	Hired Staff & Marketing	Q2	-	-	-	-
Establish & Implement Market Launch Plan	Marketing	Q2	-	$20,000	-	-
Launch Operation	Assign Staff	Q2	-	$250,000	$700,000	52%

STRATEGY #3 ~ Establish Sample Repository Serving the San Francisco Bay Market

TACTIC	RESPONSIBILITY	TIME FRAME	ADD TO STAFF	COST	PROJECTED REVENUE	GROSS MARGIN%
Establish Formal Strategic Alliance with "D" Corporation	Assign Staff	Q1	-	-	-	-
Identify & Lease Operating Facility	Assign Staff	Q2	-	$150,000	-	-
Hire & Train Facility Staff	Assign Staff	Q3	3	$180,000	-	-
Establish & Implement Standard Operating Procedures	Hired Staff & Marketing	Q2	-	-	-	-
Establish & Implement Market Launch Plan	Marketing	Q2	-	$20,000	-	-
Launch Operation	Assign Staff	Q3	-	$350,000	$700,000	52%

through the sale of the companies), or, if it is a publicly owned company, it refers to the growth in the cumulative value of its stock.

Your strategic plan is the loom upon which you weave the tapestry of your Vision. It will articulate your affirmations, cultivate organizational presence, and enable you, as the leader, to employ a tool that continuously measures effectiveness. You will find that its very structure will enable flexibility in execution and accommodate shifts due to unforeseen, emerging opportunities. In the end, it is your story of success.

~ Key Concepts

- Strategic planning is the articulation of increasingly specific affirmations of creative visualization.

- Goals, by reflecting your Vision, should be bold and grand. They are the visualization of where you want to be in three to five years yet are written as if they have already come into being.

- Objectives need to be measurable in terms of achievement and timeframe. The step-by-step attainment of your Objectives will drive you towards the achievement of your goals.

- Strategies are the initiatives that enable the attainment of your Objectives. Strategies guide your positioning, pricing, marketing, public relations, and operations.

- Tactics are the day-to-day activities that implement your Strategies. Tactics are a key tool in keeping associates focused in the present.
- Your Strategic Plan should be a living document. As it is implemented, feedback mechanisms should be put in place to calibrate company activities to optimize market activities.
- Your Strategic Plan tells the story of your company.

~ Exercise

Establish a Goal based upon your Vision. Set three Objectives that will move you closer to attaining your Goal. Explore the Strategies you will need to initiate to achieve your Objectives. Create a step-by-step Tactical plan to implement your strategies. Monitor and measure your progress over the next several months and see if this exercise contributes to your organization's momentum.

Chapter Eight ~
Creating and Sustaining a Conscious Culture

"The only real voyage consists not in seeking new landscapes, but in having new eyes; in seeing the universe through the eyes of another, one hundred others - in seeing the hundred universes that each of them sees."
Marcel Proust

The most enlightened vision, the most elegant strategy requires the positive energy of a team in continuous alignment with the actions and intentions of aligned purpose. In today's world, where value creation emerges from intellectual property, human beings have never been more central to success. The business community is slowly evolving in their understanding of the importance of human beings as the drivers of sustainable performance.

This is reflected in the jargon. What were once *Personnel Departments* became *Human Resources*, and *HR* is now evolving towards *Talent Management*. While this line of thinking shows promise there often still exists a disconnection between posturing and jargon and the actions of leadership.

This slow march still leaves many organizations far from embracing the complex, nuanced, and multi-dimensional nature of human beings. We are much more than an amalgamation of our cognitive abilities, education, and accumulation of experiences. And yet, for the most part, that's exactly the criteria most commonly associated with recruitment and hiring.

The fact is, there is something *accretive* about our very nature. A fully actualized human being represents a sum that is greater than his or her individual attributes, talents, experiences, and education. There is something beyond this mere accounting, something mysterious and beautiful. Something that sparks the creativity that lies within us all!

Our ability to connect, engage, and authentically motivate others emerges through our emotional competencies, often referred to as *emotional intelligence*. This refers to our self-awareness, social awareness, self-management, and relationship management skills. Research reveals that more than 80% of success in life can be attributed to the level of emotional *self mastery* that emerges through the development of these abilities. The remaining 20% relates to our native intelligence and cognitive abilities.

Perhaps the single most important *sensor-connector* in the human experience (and one critical to effective leadership) is our ability to express empathy.   Again, an ability that emerges through our emotional attunement. Contemporary business culture tends to ask us to leave our emotions at home.   Yet, in doing so, they are disconnecting us from our very nature.   Leaving our hearts on the sidelines disengages us from both our employers and our authentic selves.

This leads us to consider the mysterious source of human creativity.   What is the source of inspiration in human beings? I venture to say it emerges from a place far beyond the mere components of our physical existence. There is something Divine in our ability to create. Something that relates to our accretive nature, of how our mind, heart, and spirit intertwine and create the essence of our *being*. To compartmentalize our gifts, to ask us for one while discounting another leaves us fragmented, less than what we are meant to be.

As I write this **IBM®** just released their 2010 Global CEO Study.   In canvasing more than 1,500 CEOs from around the world, a revelation came to light. According to these business leaders, the single most important leadership competency necessary for success in the future is creativity. Not managerial discipline, mental rigor, integrity, or vision...but creativity. They go on to identify the solution to this challenge lies in cultivating creativity throughout the entire organization. This is a hopeful sign. An acknowledgement that the driver of success going forward must embrace the creative nature of human beings.

Unfortunately, the mindset in today's workplace is often one of fear. Fear from leadership to acknowledge our authentic nature. Fear with associates to take risks with positive intention. Fear based in a lack of trust and the insecurities rooted in ego-driven behavior.

The historical lack of commitment from many businesses towards associates has instilled an incessant, negative expectation. Waiting for the other shoe to drop. Leading associates to hedge their emotional and energetic contributions, protecting their themselves by projecting a false façade. Managers defend territory and take issues personally. Doesn't *feel* like a creative place, does it?

Fortunately, it is not imperative to speak of the authentic nature of humans to acknowledge, embrace, and cultivate the creative potential of human beings. However, in many environments, a conscious break in the perspective and behavior of leadership needs to occur for creativity to emerge. Creativity is tough to manufacture...it needs to be coaxed out. I think you can see how it takes a different mindset and perspective to spark a creative environment.

The philosophy of winning at any cost has become deeply rooted in many corporate settings. The attitude of *if we're not growing, we're dying* has always befuddled me to a certain degree. I'm not speaking of small, growing businesses trying to build traction or mid-size companies moving quickly to leverage capabilities. I mean some of the really large businesses I've worked for in the past. Growth tells one part of the story, but I've seen some areas where less would have been more both in the near term and strategically for the organization. Moving forward isn't always a linear process.

Be smart here. Learn to measure your steps towards progress in the tangible motion of the business. Are you positioning your talent, capabilities, and culture in a position poised for *adaptability*? This is what the CEOs in the survey are concerned about...finding the creative thinkers that can navigate this new horizon.

~ Reaping What Has Been Sown

Businesses have a difficult time addressing things they cannot measure, yet there are real costs associated with these veiled issues. The greatest hidden cost that erodes organizational performance is employee disengagement. Gallup®, Inc. has been measuring employee engagement levels since the beginning of the decade and reports on these surveys in the Gallup Management Journal. The study indicates 29% of employees in America are engaged (meaning they work with passion, energy, and are emotionally connected to their organization), 56% of employees are not engaged (meaning they are physically present but do not work with passion or energy), and 15% are actively disengaged (meaning they actually are working at cross purpose with their fellow associates). The study estimates the annual, aggregate cost of employee disengagement is anywhere between $237 and $270 billion in lost productivity.[17] A recent study published in the Harvard Business Review® indicates that during what is

---

[17] The Gallup Management Journal, New York, NY, October 12, 2006.

now termed The Great Recession the percentage of actively disengaged employees has skyrocketed to 21%![18]

If we extrapolate these findings into a small business environment (even using the conservative numbers from Gallop), say one with twenty employees and payroll of $1 million, the impact of employee engagement becomes strikingly tangible.

In this scenario we can anticipate six employees are activity engaged, eleven are sleepwalking through their day, and three are actively working to undermine the company's mission. If we give the sleepwalkers the benefit of the doubt, that they're perhaps contributing at 50% of their capabilities, we can assume that at a minimum, $425,000 of our million dollar payroll is providing no return on investment whatsoever. This doesn't take into account the value the actively disengaged employees are actually destroying through their efforts beyond the lost wages we are paying them. Conversely, we are only enjoying a full return on investment on thirty percent of our annual payroll through our associates that are actively and passionately engaged with the mission!

_____

[18] "How to Keep Your Top Talent", Harvard Business Review, May 2010.

Thankfully, the intentions and congruent actions of authentic leadership can re-engage many of the sleepwalkers by cultivating an atmosphere of trust and inclusion.

The fifteen to twenty-one percent that are working to undermine their fellow associates simply need to go. Their participation in the enterprise frustrates passionate associates and serves to foment further disengagement with the sleepwalkers. This is a great example of addition through subtraction.

Creating a shift in culture to one of trust and engagement begins with authenticity; the suspension of managerial ego in the daily interaction of the business. Altruistic intentions combined with congruent actions resonates positive energy and engages associates to be fully present and contributory. A genuine concern for the well being of associates that is consistently expressed will ignite the collective consciousness of a fully present team.

You'd be surprised how quickly leadership can turn around associate disengagement. In the 1990's I was working as the Vice President of International Marketing for a major medical device company. My responsibilities brought me into close and frequent contact with the

European managing directors for each country we operated in throughout the continent. Moral was very low as the corporation historically had operated as a classic U.S. exporter into the region. Products, services, pricing, and business methods were not tailored for the individual cultures and markets. Everything was developed and dictated from the U.S. corporate office. This situation was exacerbated by a veritable turnstile of senior management being assigned from the states that was not sensitive to the various cultural and operational nuances that existed country to country and quite often within the nation states themselves.

The first thing I did as the new Vice President was to begin listening to the concerns of the managing directors and repositioning our portfolio to more closely align with their particular business needs. This quickly escalated into my advocating with corporate the need to begin manufacturing products in Europe for Europeans and to expand our services within each market. The European associates began to witness my actions matching my words and a new found faith in the future of the organization began to emerge. For the first time in years the European associates began to feel the company aligning with their interests, markets, and corresponding opportunities for career success.

Within a few short months I found myself promoted to Vice President of Sales and Marketing for Europe, Africa, and the Middle East. Not only was I faced with the challenge of relating to a wide spectrum of cultural perspectives but I was also twenty years younger than all of my direct reports (European hierarchies tend to move much slower than U.S. companies when it comes to promotions). With my new level of authority I began empowering the managing directors to conduct business in the manner that best suited their opportunities and constraints. I knew I had secured their trust when my managing director for Eastern Europe and the Middle East, Thanassis Bouzabardis, spoke up during a business dinner in Madrid with all of the managing directors, "Terry, I think I can speak for all of the directors when I tell you we don't view you as another American coming here to manage our business...we view you as a fellow European."

To this day I feel that was one of the greatest complements I've ever received regarding my leadership style and abilities. By listening, expressing authentic empathy for their environments, and acting congruently I began shifting the culture of the business from a place of poor morale to re-engaging the European associates. All of this took place within six short months. The European team also increased sales by more than $16 million in that same timeframe!

Early stage companies have the advantage of starting with a relatively blank slate. Enlightened hiring practices will attract enlightened talent. Authentic leadership will attract authenticity. Sharing the Vision during the hiring process will help in this regard as will following one's intuition.

The compensation plan offered to new hires can also weed out people simply looking for immediate gratification versus people in search of being a part of something more meaningful and of greater significance in their lives. The compensation package can reveal if a person is looking for remuneration based solely on their perceived individual value or if they are willing to work for a reasonable, competitive wage buoyed by incentives derived through team value creation and the tangible contribution of achieving shared goals.

The courage of visionary conviction will not miss out on what may appear to be the minimum talent threshold necessary for performance. It will, in fact, reveal human beings capable of continuous growth and cooperation. Fully engaged, eclectically talented associates, build the creative bandwidth necessary for adaptive problem solving along the way.

Existing organizations are faced with a more challenging task in the cultivation of positive, collective consciousness. It cannot be achieved overnight, but through the application of authenticity and consistent, conscious leadership it can happen in a surprisingly short period of time as my experience in Europe proved. The expression of empathy combined with the vibrant cultivation of trust can rehabilitate the most disengaged workforce in a few short months.

Supported by honest accountability, starting with self-accountability, a conscious leader will begin to engage associates that have developed conditioned behaviors of self-preservation that dilute creative contribution. The onus is on the leader to reach out and begin to display and communicate their dedication to the well being of each individual on the team. Leadership that chooses to serve the team as a primary approach towards serving the business.

~ Empathy

The authentic expression of empathy contributes to our presence and is capable of re-engaging disaffected associates. Most of us, at one time or another, have worked for companies and bosses that used us for their own personal gain. I have. Not a lot of fun. The conditioned behavior of caution, of keeping our heads down and not fully and openly offering all of our gifts and talents to the endeavor is a natural result of these past experiences in the workplace. Words alone cannot heal these wounds. After all, language only represents approximately ten percent of how we communicate with other beings. Empathy comes directly from the heart and radiates an unspoken energy that is felt by those we encounter, whether they are immediately conscious of it or not. In a way, it's the energetic acknowledgement that we're all connected and share in a common human experience. By being sensitive to the emotions of others, empathy communicates authentic concern for another person's well being.

I discovered a powerful metaphor for authentic presence while working with Linda Kohanov and the Epona herd of horses at her ranch in Arizona. One of the early phases of the Epona Approach™ involves an exercise called the reflective round pen. As prey animals, horses are natural empaths; they acutely feel the emotions and intention of those around them. They sense emotion as information, information they receive from the intelligence centers in their enormous hearts and guts. This is an evolutionary survival mechanism in prey animals. They don't stop to mentally analyze or judge these messages. To pause and think about what they're feeling may lead to their becoming a predator's next meal.

Horses trust these messages and act without hesitation. The empathic powers of horses are so finely tuned that when they encounter a human that is incongruent (displaying behavior that doesn't match their intention) the horse will quietly walk away. They feel beyond the masks we humans so often wear with each other. Conversely, if the horse feels a person is congruent with their emotions, good, bad, or, indifferent, they will join up with them. People are very similar. Leaders that are capable of maintaining presence and radiate congruency of intention and emotion will see their constituents wanting to join up with them as well.

Linda prepares the person for the reflective round pen exercise with a horse by having the person conduct a body scan; a self-reflective process aimed at reconnecting the person with the intelligence centers that exist in their body as well as their head. It is an exercise in presence that enables the participant to focus on what they are feeling within their entire being, reconnecting with the messages our body is continuously attempting to send us. By connecting with our whole body intelligence we can begin to get out of our head and into our heart, recognizing what we are feeling and allowing the messages these emotions are attempting to convey to us. It really is the first step in developing self mastery, being completely present within one's self. Self-awareness opens the mind to see through eyes of others.

My first experience with the reflective round pen offered several powerful revelations. First, when I conducted my body scan (I actually envision a conscious form of an MRI scanning down my body) I noticed tension in my shoulders.

Linda instructed me to acknowledge and expand this feeling and to "breathe into that sensation, sending it oxygen and awareness. Ask it what information it's holding for you and be open to how your body may speak to you."

Being a novice with horses I was a bit tense as I prepared to enter a sixty foot round pen with a 2,200 pound black Percheron named Kairos. As I followed Linda's instructions I sensed the tension in my shoulders inform me to *just relax...just be*. The moment I acknowledge this message and spoke it out loud the tension dissipated instantly. (This is a consistent occurrence using this practice. My firm, Performance Transformation, employs this experiential learning approach in our various leadership, sales, and team building workshops. We witness this *release* in more than 90% of our participants.)

I entered the round pen embodying this message, to relax and simply be present. As I did, Kairos approached me, his giant hoofs gently puffing up dust as the physical and energetic space between us narrowed. Before I knew it, his soft nose was touching my forehead, his deep, solemn breath washing over my face; in fact washing over my entire being. We began to move together around the pen in delicate synchronization. Neither he nor I was leading. Neither he nor I was following. Somehow we were perfectly connected in co-creative relationship, entirely in the moment. Our movements anticipated one another's as we stepped around the pen, side by side, without judgment or mental noise, profoundly connected in a place of peacefulness and trust.

What I had discovered was that by connecting with my embodied intelligence I had truly aligned with my self. A moment of authentic presence emerged and my ability to empathically connect with another sentient being flowed effortlessly. It seemed that Kairos and I felt each other's presence so clearly we were able to connect on a majestically beautiful and inspirational level. Neither of us attempted to dominate the other, we could simply move in the moment with grace and dignity.

The analogy of what I had experienced in leading the European business team those many years ago was not lost upon me. I had entered into the leadership relationship with an open mind and, perhaps more importantly, an open heart. I did not judge their ways of doing business as worse or better than corporate's perspective. It was simply their way of doing things that suited their markets and environment. I genuinely cared about their success and empowered them to co-create the relationship resulting in a level of acceptance and respect that still resonates with me today.

Some of us are natural empaths; capable of feeling the emotional energy of those we encounter. This can be as much of a curse as it is a blessing. Humans that are highly sensitive to these emissions can actually be overwhelmed by the emotions of those they encounter. We've all experienced this on some level. Think back to a moment when you may have encountered someone experiencing significant inner conflict; you most likely recoiled from that person without even being conscious as to why you reacted this way. You simply knew you wanted to put space between you and that person.

While it can be challenging, natural empaths are well served by learning to discern the emotional energy of others from their own. Conversely, those of us that are less aware of the emotional energy surrounding us are capable of learning how to calibrate our sensitivity to others.

I learned this while working on the empathy education company project I mentioned earlier in this book. The company used scenario-based learning for clinical health care professionals to elevate their ability to express empathy towards people and family members experiencing a health crisis.

There is a significant difference between simply being present, expressing authentic empathy, and trying to *fix* the person or situation. As we learned during this project, this is an exceptionally difficult delineation for health care providers and people drawn to serve others. They are attracted to their profession by their desire to heal people, to ease their suffering by fixing their ailment. It is difficult for them to accept there are certain situations they cannot fix, and attempting to do so beyond a certain point communicates a paternalistic, almost patronizing message to people in deep emotional pain.

What we discovered was the clinicians needed to learn to let go of this attitude and accept, what in their conditioned, well trained terms is considered defeat. In other words, accept things exactly as they are. The kindest and most conscientious expression they can offer at that point is empathy. In certain situations they can no longer heal the body yet they can still help heal the spirit.

The lesson here is that empathy does not require action, only presence, authentic listening, and the allowance of space for emotional processing. Simply being sensitive to the situations of those around us and quietly acknowledging what they may be experiencing is an expression of empathy. We all experience ups and downs in our personal lives. If leadership wants associates to be truly engaged, they must recognize these trials and tribulations will inevitably follow people into the workplace. Authenticity recognizes emotions, both highs and lows, as part of being whole and present.

~ Professional Development Plans

A powerful tool for building trust and cultivating empathy throughout the organization is the Professional Development Plan. It is a straightforward and inexpensive approach for engaging associates. Basically, it is a documented conversation regarding an associate's goals, aspirations, and perceptions. It is supported by an action plan designed to support the associate in the realization of their professional goals.

Throughout my career I have consistently been surprised by the fact I was often the first manager to introduce this process in the organization. This, in and of itself was differentiating, but what proved more important was my intention that the development plan not be constrained by the immediate goals of the organization. It was about the associate.

This approach enabled the two of us to build a bridge of open and honest communication regarding both their strengths and their professional developmental needs. The open communication removed ambiguity by providing an opportunity for the associate to assess themselves and come to understand what they needed to do to get to where they wanted to go. If they were passed up for a promotion there was a common understanding of where they were on their developmental path, thus removing their propensity to react with negative emotions of somehow being unfairly treated or unappreciated by the firm. It is another tool to help keep associates focused in the moment, not worrying about a future that may or may not come to pass, and establish a sense of empowerment over their own fate.

The first part of a Professional Development Plan is a joint assessment of where the associate is today. It is best to conduct this independently of each other, allowing ample time for reflection and consideration. Start by asking the associate to assess their current skills that enable success in their current areas of responsibility. Have them list their strengths as well as where they feel they could grow and evolve professionally.

Reinforce your support to the associate by commenting that this is not meant to judge their performance, but is intended to identify the resources the firm needs to allocate to help them grow professionally. Choose your language carefully. Be sure to keep the focus on "professional growth" so the process will not be perceived as a personal issue. Most associates will be a bit anxious at this point of the conversation, so it is important to follow it up quickly with the next phase of the planning process.

The next step is to ask them where they see themselves in five years, and again, in ten years. I always follow this up with "regardless of whether it is with us or with another company". Emphasize this is intended to place them on a path of professional growth. It may eventually lead them to explore opportunities elsewhere and that is okay!

Follow up this comment with, "Hey, you might entirely outgrow the organization and if that's what is right for you then it is nothing other than a wonderful thing!" This is where authenticity comes in as a powerful, transformational force. Let the associate know this is about their professional growth and not just an attempt to serve the company. One automatically benefits the other and it is in the best interest of the company to invest in their growth.

From here ask the associate to identify the skills they think they will need to develop in order to manifest their personal vision of professional success. Commit to providing them with an honest assessment of what your perspective is in this matter. Assure them that together, you will formulate a step-by-step program to expose them to these skills. This can be through involving them in different projects, functional teams, or through formal training and education. Even a resource constrained organization can find learning opportunities for its associates by allowing exposure to the various functional activities of the business.

Formalize the process by writing it down in a structured document that you both sign and date and identify a specific timeframe for review. At a minimum, take the time to sit down and review the document with the associate every six months with the intention of making adjustments and recording accomplishments.

By making a conscious decision to invest in the growth of your associates you will express your sincere interest in their well-being, growth, and satisfaction. I guarantee they will take the form home to their significant other and sit down and talk about the process. I can't tell you how many times I had an associate come back in to discuss the plan and comment that their wife or husband wished they had a similar process where they work!

The Professional Development Plan rounds out people's skills as well as creating awareness and empathy for their fellow associates. It sends the message that advancement comes through professional development and not through competitive behavior with fellow associates. The plan affords them the opportunity to explore other facets of the organization and to understand how the firm functions and interconnects. In this way it builds relationships throughout the entire organization.

It helps everyone see how what they do impacts others either positively or negatively. This will foster empathy and a new sense of appreciation for each other. In this way a tool intended to primarily focus on an individual's evolution actually builds camaraderie and teamwork. Most importantly, the use of Professional Development Plans communicates and affirms legitimate concern for the associate and establishes a baseline of trust and open communication.

On a very fundamental level, the Professional Development Plan addresses what psychologist Jaak Panksepp[19] identified as one of the key components of the mammalian core emotional system. Dr. Panksepp's research identified four basic emotions all mammals experience as part of our survival mechanisms. They are seeking, rage, fear, and panic.

Implementing development plans addresses our need, at the most fundamental level of our consciousness, to continuously be seeking (exploring and making sense of our environment as we move forward in our existence). Additional research indicates that the seeking, in and of itself, feels good. Experiments in this area show that the anticipation of a reward creates the same response in the brain's pleasure center as enjoying the reward itself. This is often referred to as the "Christmas Effect", referencing the joyful anticipation children feel on the approach of Christmas morning. Leaders that create environments that are conscious of our ancient, core emotional systems will help cultivate employee engagement.

---

[19] Jaak Panksepp, Affective Neuroscience: The Foundations of Human and Animal Emotions. New York: Oxford University Press, 1998.

Over time, the plans also create the foundation for succession planning. This is an area that is often overlooked until sudden pressures move an enterprise to scramble in reaction to impending leadership needs. I was recently approached by a bank that suddenly realized their mid to upper level managers were all between the ages of fifty-five and fifty-eight years old. They approached me to ask if I could help them put together a leadership development program that would lay the foundation for succession planning. The process would take the better part of a year, introduce an unanticipated additional operational expense, and take time away from the daily tasks of an already stretched management team. If the organization had been employing Professional Development Plans as part of their managerial process, all of these issues could have been avoided.

~ The Accretive Coaching Process™

The creation of Professional Development Plans is a modified form of coaching. Through this process, leadership is not attempting to provide all the answers, but is providing a mirror for professional self reflection and development. Leadership provides direct guidance as to the types of skills the associate may wish to consider developing in order to realize their own personal vision of success. The perspective of leadership will, however, inevitably be shaded by the internal objectives of the organization.

Independent, professional coaches from outside of an organization can add substantial value in building trust and improving performance in a company. This may sound strange coming from an Executive Coach, but I advise caution and due diligence when considering the engagement of a professional coach. Over the past decade, the growth of professional coaching has grown precipitously. Whenever there is a rush to the next hot revenue stream you're inevitably going to see people jumping into a profession they're ill equipped to master. Along with this growth has come a series of credentialing and professional organizations whose sole purpose is to promote the interests of its membership. Taking the time to ensure a good fit and tying the coaching engagement to tangible outcomes and measurable improvements will serve both the coaching client and the coaching profession.

The current positioning of the dominant coach certifying trade group states that coaches are not, and need not be, subject matter experts. All the answers must come from the client. The coach is simply there to facilitate this voyage of self-discovery. I don't buy into this line of thought. Would an NFL franchise hire a basketball coach to develop their football team? This person may be a coach, yes, but I think a bit of subject matter expertise is called for in this and all other situations.

It is important to remember that professional coaching emerged out of the old paradigm. Things are dramatically changing in the business world. In their book, "Leadership on the Line"[20], Ronald A. Heifetz and Marty Linsky introduce the concept of technical challenges versus adaptive challenges. When an organization is faced with a technical challenge, they already have the answers within their current level of consciousness; they know what to do...they just haven't chosen to do it.

In such cases, the traditional approach of professional coaching may, in fact, add value. Adaptive challenges go much deeper and are more likely to reflect the landscape we are currently traversing today (the seismic generational, demographic, and geographic shifts that lie at the very

---

[20] "Leadership On The Line", Ronald A. Heifetz and Marty Linsky, Harvard Business School Press, Boston, MA, 2002.

foundation of the new source of value creation – human talent).

Adaptive challenges require a shift in beliefs, culture, habits, and to a certain degree, values. This type of change can push people beyond their tolerance levels and cannot occur until a fundamental shift in perspective emerges. A heightened sense of self-awareness must be fostered, accompanied by a new set of tools for navigating the adaptive landscape. Coaching must integrate an element of education in order to navigate a landscape requiring adaptive change.

By combining coaching with educational development, significant change can be embraced and leveraged for success. A study a few years back by The Journal of Public Personnel Management indicated training improves managerial performance by approximately 25%. Training combined with coaching improves performance by 88%. It is from this perspective that we've developed a new model of professional coaching called the Accretive Coaching Process™.

While the term *accretive* may not be all that familiar in everyday parlance, it accurately describes both the intention and execution of the process. There are several definitions for the word accretive, but two resonate with me. The first refers to *an increase in natural growth or by gradual external addition* which reflects the integration of self-reflection with an educational process. The second definition refers to *the growing together of separate parts into a whole of greater value.* I especially like this definition as it addresses "separate parts", which from my perspective touches upon our hidden or untapped abilities as well as external ideas and perspectives we may have been unaware of prior to engaging in the Accretive Coaching Process™ .

The key departure Accretive Coaching takes from traditional coaching modalities lies in the active, educational aspects of the process. Over three years in development, the process intrinsically weaves education with self reflection and growth. In order to adapt and address the challenges we face today these aspects of development are inseparable.

The educational aspects of the process include traditional, didactic learning sessions. In our various leadership, sales, and team building workshops we integrate these traditional methods with experiential learning sessions based upon The Epona Approach™.[21] The Epona Approach is a series of ground-based, self reflective learning exercises conducted with horses.

Through our work assisting veterans of Iraq and Afghanistan re-assimilate to civilian life (our Warriors in Transition program received a certificate of commendation from General David Petraeus in February, 2010 for our workshops conducted in partnership with Quantum Leap Farm) we came upon two powerful realizations. First, the exercises conducted with the horses provides an interesting framework for psychologists to engage in Cognitive Behavioral Therapy with soldiers experiencing Post Traumatic Stress Disorder.[22] Second, and more relevant to our coaching process, is the fact that this approach to experiential learning strongly correlates with Professor David Kolb's discoveries in adult learning styles.

First published in 1984, Professor Kolb's work demonstrated two fascinating discoveries. First, adult learning emerges through a cycle (Kolb's Learning Cycle).

---

[21] The Epona Approach™ is an Equine Assisted Learning approach developed by Linda Kohanov.

[22] This aspect of our work was acknowledge by our invitation to present at the 18th Annual International Military and Civilian Combat Stress Conference held in May, 2010, Los Angeles, CA.

Concrete experience opens the door for reflective observation. Observations will correlate to abstract concepts, and these concepts can be tested through experimentation. The experiences garnered through

Performance Transformation's Proprietary Accretive Coaching Process™

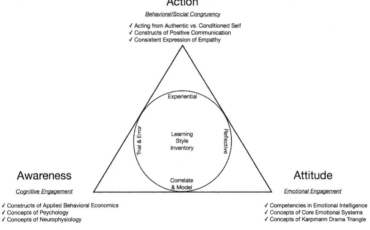

experimentation starts the cycle over again.

The facilitation of Equine Facilitated Learning exercises employed in our workshops moves seamlessly through the entire learning cycle. The unique and typically unfamiliar nature of working in partnership with a horse also lowers the barriers to learning, placing people at the edge of their comfort zone in a safe, enjoyable manner.

The facilitation of the process helps participants frame and correlate the unique, self reflective experience (connecting and communicating non-verbally with the horse) with concepts relating to how they solve problems, communicate, and motivate fellow associates, customers, and subordinates in real life. The participants not only observe each other, but interact and see how they conduct themselves in challenging, unfamiliar circumstances (adaptive challenges).

From this shift in perspective (which is hard to avoid), people can experiment with different approaches to problem solving, communication, cooperation, and leadership without the need to dominate or coerce the horse. In all my years of leadership experience and coaching this approach to experiential learning is the single most powerful tool I've seen for creating a positive shift in perspective, opening the door for sustainable professional development and personal growth.

The second pillar of Kolb's seminal work is the discovery of the Learning Style Inventory. Individuals have a particular style of learning. Kolb's Learning Style Inventory identifies four common styles for learning:

✓ Diverging ~ A style exemplified by feeling and watching (Concrete Experience and Reflective Observation).

✓ Assimilating ~ A style exemplified by watching and thinking (Reflective Observation and Abstract Conceptualization).

✓ Converging ~ A style exemplified by doing and thinking (Active Experimentation and Abstract Conceptualization).

✓ Accommodating ~ A style exemplified by doing and feeling (Active Experimentation and Concrete Experience).

This explains what we've witnessed incorporating the exercises with the horses. Regardless of a particular participant's learning style, the process moves them through the entire learning cycle. It literally speaks to everyone! Woven throughout the experiential learning process are competencies in Emotional Intelligence[23], the constructs of Applied Behavioral Economics[24], along with

---

[23] Based upon the research of Dr. Daniel Goleman, Dr. Peter Salovey, Dr. John Mayer, and their colleagues.

[24] Based in large part upon the research of Dr. Dan Ariely.

concepts from psychology (Core Emotional Systems[25]), and recent discoveries from neurophysiology[26].

Accretive Coaching is designed addresses the mind, heart and spirit. It cultivates self-awareness through self reflection, which opens the door for a shift in inner and outer perspective to occur. Once this shift is experienced, emotional fitness tools are introduced affording people the opportunity to be fully present with their thoughts and feelings. The process places people in touch with other sources of information and knowledge our socially conditioned selves often ignore or overlook. This enhanced awareness, what the philosopher Christian de Quincy calls *feeling our thinking*[27], enables us to traverse the adaptive journey, discovering new ways of being and doing along the way.

Accretive Coaching is highly transformational. As a leadership development tool it cultivates deep self

---

[25] Based upon the research of Dr. Jaak Paksepp.

[26] Based upon the research of Dr. C. Marci, Dr. J. Armour, Dr. G. Stroink, Dr. R. McCraty, Dr. R. Levenson et al, Dr. M. Iacoboni, and Dr. M. Csikszentmihalyi.

[27] "Radical Knowing, Understanding Consciousness Through Relationship", Christian de Quincey, Park Street Press, Rochester, Vermont, 2005.

discovery and accelerates the path towards heightened empathy and authenticity. It propels teams (especially teams of knowledge workers) to new levels of creative cooperation and alignment with authentic organizational culture. For people that desire to be elsewhere, this process

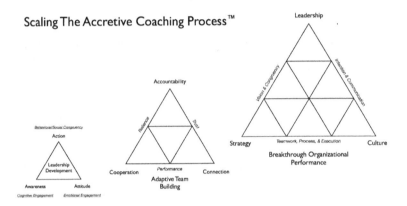

will assist them in finding the courage to do so. Associates that desire being a part of the team will become more trusting, present, and will flourish. The associates that align with your authentic culture will naturally emerge and those that do not feel this alignment will matriculate out of the enterprise. This results in the enterprise engaging the right people doing the right things at the right time that contribute to the organization's goals.

~ Authentic Discourse, Authentic Culture

Cultivating open and honest discourse throughout the organization supports a community of trust. Leadership should engage their associates in authentic conversations regarding the progress and challenges of the business. No single person has all the answers, but collectively any question or concern can be addressed. Encourage associates to challenge the assumptions of leadership. This reflects an attitude of respect and inclusion and serves the interests of the firm.

Associates are quite often much closer to the customer and are immersed in the daily, critical processes that deliver value to the marketplace. Inclusion is not a sign of weakness, but a display of enlightenment and strength. Authentic leaders do not fear open and honest questions. Managers dominated by their ego fear being questioned, and often react vociferously in order to maintain their dominance over the organization. This type of reaction drives associates underground and disengages them from being fully present at work. Remember, it is not important that the leader always be right. It is, however, imperative that the company be right and that the associates engage fully in the process.

Involving the entire organization in a continuous, productive discourse builds confidence and a sense of empowerment. Open communication enables organizations to share knowledge across traditionally isolated silos of operation. Leadership sets the tone through their suspension of ego, removing territorial boundaries within the enterprise, and by tapping into the entire continuum of human capabilities. Ideas for innovation in one area may come from another.

By embracing everyone's participation a new energy emerges throughout the collective consciousness. The intention is to better serve customers, not to protect egos, fiefdoms, or individual insecurities. By elevating the conversation to continuously focus on the customer, leadership can direct attention away from petty issues that not only fail to contribute value to the enterprise, but actually cause erosion.

The suspension of ego cultivates the awareness of authentic self. This in turn propagates intuition, creativity, and the security that can only come through the perennial knowledge that resides in the heart. It evaporates organizational fear that is a learned behavior of the socially conditioned self. Think for a moment about the hidden productivity that is continuously siphoned off through endemic political posturing. Numerous market research studies indicate that associates spend less than half their time on the job pursuing activities that actually create value for their companies! Insecure and fearful employees engage in passive aggressive behavior either to gain what they perceive as an advantage over a fellow associate or to protect the imaginary territories they've created in their minds. Is it any wonder why enlightened companies achieve breakthrough performance? They have unleashed the hidden workforce that exists within their midst! The cultivation of authenticity in the business culture alleviates the burden of fear, easily doubling the productivity of associates.

Over time, the emerging culture of authenticity will resonate to dislodge the negativity of passive aggressive behavior. Such behavior simply becomes unacceptable within the enterprise and people that choose to engage in it lose their power to intimidate and control fellow associates. Again, it starts with leadership setting the tone of authenticity, positive behavior, and open communication.

Passive aggressive behavior cannot thrive in an environment of genuine intention and openness. This environment will naturally help people that choose not to adapt to the new culture to matriculate to other organizations where their modus operandi still serves their mindset. A culture of authenticity eventually becomes self sustaining. A multiplier effect emerges as the positive attitudes of the organizational culture resonates beyond the brick and mortar of the enterprise to engage customers, associates, and partners that embrace the enlightened Vision.

~ Aligning Interests

A very powerful indicator to associates of how they are appreciated is in the way they are compensated. This resonates deeply with how they feel about the organization as it validates their sense of worth and clearly reflects how leadership feels about their value to the team. Notice I am using the term feels rather than thinks. Compensation can be a highly emotional issue. People don't decide to leave an organization because they think they are under-appreciated. They leave because they feel they are under-appreciated. Conversely, humans will give more of themselves if they feel their contributions are truly embraced and appreciated by the enterprise.

Being fully present means being open and contributory from the mind as well as the heart. This intention is clearly felt by customers who engage in transactions with a company. My success as a salesperson was directly related to the relationships I developed with my customers. People do business with people they like, with people they feel have their interest at heart.

In this age of hyper-competitive business, most products and services that are in final consideration by a prospect will all serve their purpose on a fairly equal basis. It is why salespeople are taught to focus on benefits rather than features. How an organization communicates the benefits it delivers to a prospect differentiates it from the competition. Companies communicate through their associates; through their presence with their prospects. The intention of leadership resonates through this conduit directly to the customers. If associates feel they are delivering real and tangible benefits for their customers, value that will fairly compensate and benefit all involved, this energy will be felt by the customer. If associates feel they are simply a delivery tool intended to enrich the company chances are this intention will be felt by the customer as well.

Compensation doesn't need to bankrupt a company; sometimes a small economic gesture amplifies intention more than a major year-end bonus. Early in my management career I had hired a young salesman that was to be married a few months into his employment with the company. He would not have qualified for paid time off at the time of his honeymoon, which was already planned, when he came to work for us. He was so positive and present with our client base that when the time came for his honeymoon I made sure he was paid for the time he was away. He came into my office upon his return with his pay stub and pointed out there must have been a mistake as he knew he wasn't eligible for the paid time off. I told him it wasn't a mistake; think of it as a wedding present from the company, a thank you for the wonderful work he was contributing to the organization. From his reaction, you would have thought I had given him a million dollars!

As newlyweds, two weeks pay was a significant issue for the young couple and the gesture was above and beyond what they had expected. He went on to become our best salesperson and a leader within the organization. The small financial gesture from the perspective of the company was a major gesture from the perspective of the associate and his wife. At a very special time in their lives the organization extended a gesture from the heart which touched them deeply. I can assure you, it came back many times over in the years that followed!

Many companies employ the use of stock options in order to align interests throughout the enterprise. While this can be a wonderful way to build long-term wealth, the intention can be a bit disingenuous. For one thing, it doesn't cost the company anything to grant options. Options are granted at a strike price; they are simply a right to purchase stock at a specified trading price, often the trading price on the day they are granted. They have no value unless the stock price escalates, which is the inferred promise in granting the option. If you contribute to the growth of the company you will share in the rewards.

The shortcoming of intention here is there is often little associates can do to influence the stock price in publicly traded markets. Long-term economic cycles, interest rates, investor preferences in investment sectors, global events, and the decisions of leadership will often have a much greater influence over the price of a stock than the day-to-day performance of associates. When incentive compensation is too highly weighted towards options it can actually be a disincentive to front line associates. I've experienced this first hand watching my false sense of prosperity evaporate as the paper value of tens of thousands of dollars that took years of hard work to accumulate plunge to less than the original strike price in a few short weeks due to a fickle stock market. I was left feeling disengaged from my ability to influence my personal prosperity regardless of the value I had contributed over years of dedicated work. I wasn't alone in this feeling as the tone of the entire company soured over the coming months.

There's another false intention that is clearly expressed by the other name for stock options; golden handcuffs. While options are granted at a strike price, they often vest over a four year term. In other words, while the options were granted at a point in time, they cannot be exercised until they have vested. This can trap people into staying with a company when their heart is no longer present.

Often, there is a very positive reason someone wishes to leave a company that in the long-run will benefit everyone involved. Handcuffing an associate to an organization that they no longer wish to be a part of simply so they can enjoy a financial gain created from past performance can be highly corrosive to the culture. The associate that wanted to leave for greener pastures may feel stuck and disengage emotionally from their work. They're just riding it out until they can cash out and get on with their life. Fellow associates pick up on this intention and lack of positive energy. This can also create a log-jam that prevents associates that desire and deserve to ascend to greater levels of responsibility in the enterprise to do so in a timely manner. It opens the door for even more people to feel stuck and to disengage from their daily presence. Handcuffs can be just that, restraints to the natural flow of an enterprise.

Aligning interests through associate ownership participation is powerful if it is done with honest intention. If stock ownership is deemed the way to go then consider granting blocks of stock rather than stock options. Create an employee stock purchasing plan. Or simpler yet, develop a profit sharing plan for the enterprise. The alignment of interest should align with the timeframe in which value is being created. A basic human premise of justice is strongly aligned with timeliness. Deferring the rewards of positive behavior too long can dilute the reinforcement of incentives and draw attention out of the present moment.

Performance incentives tied directly to revenue generation can either align or disconnect an organization. I am often surprised by leaders that fear variable compensation that is paid upon performance. Working as a consultant with emerging companies I have seen owners that refuse to offer open ended commission programs for salespeople. When the issue is discussed they often voice concerns that they're too small a company; they simply cannot afford to pay their sales force such high commissions. This is truly backward thinking. Commissions are paid after the revenue has been generated and profits created, so they don't actually cost the company anything. If the revenue and profit aren't delivered no commissions are paid. The fact is, many of the most successful companies embrace this concept of variable compensation on performance.

Enlightened leadership should celebrate the fact that their revenue generators are making exceptional livings! There was once a time when leaving the sales force to take a job in management meant taking a pay cut. It was seen as making an investment in one's professional growth. Once upon a time, and I know this is hard to comprehend in this day of grossly overpaid executives, the best salespeople in a company made more money than the president of the company! Unfortunately, the ego of many business leaders has evolved to a point where compensation throughout organizations is highly out of balance.

Another key attribute for aligning interests is to tie incentives generated through revenue and profit creation throughout the value continuum of the entire organization. Remarkably successful salespeople may look like lone wolves, but there are significant support personnel behind the scenes that enable their success.

Companies often divide their associates into two classes of people; revenue generators and overhead. This is driven by an internally focused culture, one that results from organizing resources around traditional perceptions of business functions. By organizing around the customers' needs this perception quickly appears artificial and superfluous. Support staff is the infrastructure necessary to efficiently deliver value to the customer and should benefit from their creative contribution. Aligning interests removes the internal silos that create an "us versus them" attitude and alleviates the need for departments to defend their perceived territory. The antiquated hierarchical organizational structure that emerged during the industrial revolution sustains this tendency and we'll discuss new paradigms of thought and structure in the next chapter.

~ "Thank You"

One of the simplest, yet most overlooked contributors to creating a positive culture is the expression of appreciation. Taking the time to say "thank you, you're doing a great job" cost nothing and resonates positive intention throughout the entire organization. Acknowledgement in front of an associate's peers can elevate this positive attitude to an even higher level.

Leadership is often quick to express their expectations and very slow to acknowledge a job well done. Expressing gratitude is a fundamental quality of conscious leadership. Gratitude for the contribution of others is another facet of empathy. It reflects leadership's consciousness of our natural human desire for validation and appreciation. Even the most stressful of times in challenging environments can be relaxed through the expression of gratitude.

An empirical and remarkably fascinating example of the power of praise is illustrated in the research of Dr.

Masaru Emoto.[28] In his research, Dr. Emoto exposes water to both the spoken and written word; words of praise as well as critical language. The water exposed to positive language is then frozen and results in the formation of beautiful, symmetric crystals. The water exposed to negative words freeze into deformed crystals. It is a fascinating representation of the power of positive intention transmitted through language. As human beings are composed of more than seventy percent water it isn't a stretch to see how we are affected in similar ways.

Challenging situations are best handled with positive language as well. Missed performance gates, underachievement, and passive aggressive behavior could be communicating issues that may be readily addressed through honest discourse and encouraging support. Even if an associate is unhappy in their current situation, a positive approach that places their interests at the forefront may lead to resolution for all involved. By approaching the most difficult situations with positive intention, leadership can reinforce the creative culture of an organization.

---

[28] "The Miracle of Water", Masaru Emoto, Atria Books, New York, NY, 2007.

Organizations transitioning from a traditional culture towards an enlightened culture will inevitably incur situations for friction to emerge, especially with associates uncomfortable with the evolving environment. This is quite natural, and should be embraced as a positive sign of the enterprise moving forward. As the transition takes hold certain behaviors will indicate discomfort with the change from certain associates. By addressing these issues in a timely and positive manner, pathways to resolution will quickly emerge. If an organization can afford a short period of transition and an unhappy associate has not acted in an unethical manner, providing an exit strategy for the associate to move on will greatly benefit the enterprise and enhance the culture.

~ Key Concepts

- Employee disengagement is rampant in the majority of companies. It saps organizations of more than half of their potential productivity.
- Empathy matters. Genuinely caring about associates is the single most powerful attribute of authentic leadership.

- Professional Development Plans are a simple, cost effective way to engage associates' minds, hearts, and spirits.
- Professional coaching can have a breakthrough impact on performance, but it can also have serious limitations. Choose coaches wisely.
- Authentic communication is a two way street. Cultivating open, honest feedback builds trust and engages associates.
- Aligning interests through compensation is a powerful leadership tool. Be timely, be genuine.
- The expression of gratitude costs nothing and can be one of the most powerful tools to engage associates.

~ Exercise

Conduct a Professional Development Plan for yourself. Where can you grow and improve your leadership skills to more effectively engage your associates?

The Transformational Entrepreneur

Chapter Nine ~
Structure and Execution

"Problems cannot be solved by the same level of thinking that created them." Albert Einstein

We've explored leadership, strategic planning, and culture as key drivers of sustainable success within a high-performance enterprise. The final two pieces of the puzzle are organizational structure and execution. How we structure the organization is a reflection of how we perceive function, and once established, how we function is highly influenced by our organizational structure.

Traditional, hierarchical business structure was developed to optimize economies of scale that served basic and heavy manufacturing during the early part of the twentieth century. Alfred Sloan, the innovative leader of General Motors in the early 1920's, is often attributed as being the father of the modern corporation due to his work in developing hierarchical structures, vertical integration (manufacturing every component that went into an automobile), and the modern use of advertising and brand management. During the recent Great Recession, GM narrowly escaped bankruptcy. Even with an infusion of billions of dollars of taxpayers' money the General Motors that Alfred Sloan knew is struggling to reinvent itself. As this massive failure unwinds experts will gather around the wreckage and attempt to ascertain what caused this colossal debacle. I anticipate they will point to highly expensive, rigid labor, bad marketing, failure of leadership to anticipate escalating gasoline prices, and their interdependency with GMAC Financial. While all of these facets were contributory, I strongly believe much of General Motors' crisis was due to its hierarchical structure that locked it into patterns of thought and behavior that hobbled its ability to evolve in these rapidly changing times.

I think it is safe to say most of us have worked for highly structured, command-and-control organizations that demanded compliance and conformity. But how many of us have worked in organizations that embraced a different approach to organizational structure and management? Even those of us that have worked in small start-up companies where structure was loose and creativity flowed, we most likely experienced the inevitable march towards traditional corporate structure as the company gained traction in the marketplace. If a new, conscious approach to leading a business is to take root, an accompanying new structure for organizing the business must follow suit. Without the accompanying shift in physical and functional structure, the patterns, behaviors, and thought processes of the old paradigm with seep through and threaten the emerging intention.

~ Conduit Structure

While conducting market research in 2005 I became intrigued with the concept of convergence; of how biotechnology, information technology, and nanotechnology were coming together to create a new generation of products and capabilities. As I discovered compelling opportunities to converge companies with specific core competencies to create breakthrough technologies I also saw barriers that would challenge this vision. The barriers emerged from two areas; Company hierarchical structure resulting in silos that challenge internal coordination (never mind external convergence); and the intellectual horsepower of Ph.D.'s that were remarkably expert in their area of application but were no more insightful than a college science graduate in the complementary technologies. From an investor's perspective, how could one converge the silos and create an environment of cross-pollination of the science and technology? The answer came to me visually and was a bit of an epiphany...lay the silos down upon their sides and introduce structural, cultural, and operational porosity to the previously isolated silos. In effect, overlap and transform them into horizontal conduits of cooperative, customer-centric, developmental process drawn together by a surrounding conduit of leadership, finance, and shared operational infrastructure.

The seeds of thought for this new structural approach germinated while consulting with Kevin Schimelfenig, Founder and Managing Partner of SalesForce4Hire®, LLC. Kevin's company provides custom sales solutions for medical device and life science organizations. The company creates custom business engines that can be absorbed or dissolved by the client and operates with a core management and talent team that expands and contracts in accordance with the needs of the current client mix. The core management team is highly cooperative and works together to move their clients' projects through a proprietary commercialization process. The focus is on process flow and the company's differentiating value highly depends upon the efficiency and speed of value creation.

In effect, the process is driven through a value creating pipeline. This value conduit is highly porous operationally, absorbing contract resources as they are needed and releasing them upon conclusion of a project. SalesForce4Hire maniacally focuses on their core competencies and outsources everything else. There are no hierarchies or silos that could place a drag on value creation or introduce the risk of becoming distracted by non-value creating activities.

Conduit Business Structure

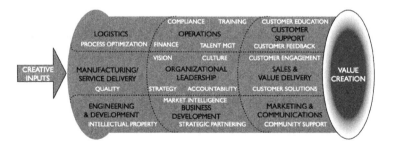

Interestingly, as I began refining the conduit structure business model I discovered, quite by accident, the root meaning of the word "conduit". The word conduit originates from the Medieval Latin conductus, from the

Latin, past participle of condūcere, meaning "to lead together". Many people say there are no coincidences, and I couldn't think of a more appropriate definition reflecting the intention of this approach to organizational structure!

I was recently consulting with an innovative, start-up medical device company that has adopted the conduit structure right out of the gate. The founder and developer of the company's technology, an M.D./Ph.D., recognized his core competencies and decided to focus on what he did best, clinical product development. The enterprise has hired an exceptional engineering firm to develop the product and optimize manufacturing processes. They've contracted expertise in F.D.A. compliance, strategic planning, and custom sales development.

As the move for their next round of funding, the company is presenting investors with a remarkably attractive asset. The dollars invested will go towards bringing the product to market with a minimal amount of overhead. Money will fund F.D.A. compliance, the manufacturing of inventory, marketing, and sales with only a small percentage allocated to compensate the core leadership team. Investors are not being asked to invest in hierarchy or brick and mortar.

This places the enterprise in a distinctly advantageous position as potential investors evaluate competing opportunities. The lack of overhead will also benefit the organization as they look to exit the business through the sale of the product line to a larger, established medical device company. They will be presenting a surprisingly clean transactional opportunity in which the only thing a potential suitor is buying is the assets they desire – the product line. This alleviates many of the potentially messy and expensive entanglements of unwinding duplicate resources. Not only does the conduit structure create a competitive advantage at the outset it also delivers significant, comparable value at exit.

My own company, Performance Transformation, LLC, employs a similar, highly efficient structure. Our core leadership team is focused on continuously moving the organization forward in the creation of value for our client base. With each engagement, we tailor the mix of resources necessary to deliver the particular solution bundle for the client. We've cultivated a network of partners and affiliates that enables us to deliver our services throughout the United States and the Europe without carrying excessive overhead. We can expand or contract in response to our clients' needs and demands. Our core competencies emerge from our conduit, but our strengths are leveraged and weaknesses addressed through our nimble delivery arms. This approach has dramatically broadened our bandwidth and flexibility without adding fixed costs. Variable expenses track directly to the variability of demand. Fixed expenses are solely focused on the continuous cultivation of our core competencies.

Both SalesForce4Hire and Performance Transformation had the advantage of never having built hierarchical organizational structures in the first place. This approach enabled the organizations to move through The Great Recession with relatively little disruption and positioned the companies to rapidly hit the accelerator with the economic recovery. The conduit structure also empowers rapid flexibility, anticipating and leading change in the marketplace as apposed to reacting and scrambling to meet the unprecedented, continuous change that is now, and will continue to be, the norm.

~ Execution

At the end of the day success in business comes down to execution. Traditionally, the old adage, if you can't measure it, your can't manage it, guided management. There's significant truth in this statement. I've witnessed expenses come under control by simply providing visibility of the expenditures to managers. Becoming aware of something initiates the management of it (this is true with self-awareness as well...it is the first step in Self Mastery). Establishing a set of metrics that are cogent to the mission is a critical step in execution. But just what should we be measuring?

Determining what to measure and how to measure it, while seemingly straightforward on the surface, can introduce unanticipated elements and results. On the surface, measuring customer satisfaction appears to be a gold standard metric, and one that has been adhered to for decades. A closer look, however, indicates how fallible this measurement actually is in the real world. The emerging discipline of Applied Behavioral Economics underscores how many of our assumptions based in neo-classical economics simply aren't true.

A 2009 research study conducted by Gallup® indicates measuring customer satisfaction can create a false sense of success and security.[29]   The report states that rationally satisfied customers are no more likely to spend more with a vendor or stay loyal to a vendor than customers that are dissatisfied. That's quite a statement. The difference lies in creating emotionally satisfied customers, customers that feel a strong connection with their vendor and have passion for their products or services.

The consensus among leading behavioral economists points to a rather unsettling fact for traditional businesses that operate along the assumptions provided by neo-classical economics: Economic decisions are roughly 70% emotional and 30% rational. How customers feel about purchases are more than twice as important as what they think about the purchase. This changes everything!

A great example of a company that thoroughly understands this is Apple. Apple has cultivated legions of fans (remember, fan is short for fanatic) that literally are willing to line up to buy their latest gadget. The company sold a million iPads in its first twenty-eight days on the market even though the initial product offered relatively limited improvements over existing technologies. That's

---

[29] "The Next Discipline - Applying Behavioral Economics to Drive Growth and Profitability" Gallup, Inc. 2009.

nearly a half billion dollars in incremental revenue within a month! Did these customers rationally need an iPad or did they emotionally desire the device? I think the answer is obvious.

Regardless of what we've been taught and conditioned to believe, emotions matter in business. The businesses that understand and embrace this are poised to pull away from the pack. In the hyper-competitive marketplace of the 21st century, understanding and applying this reality may be the key differentiator between competing organizations. Emotions, and the emotional intelligence of associates, has a major influence on what is measured and how relative the statistical analysis is to the reality of the business.

I witnessed this phenomena while working as the Vice President of Sales and Marketing for a life science company. Our V.P. of Manufacturing was a rather bombastic, highly dominant gentleman that had matriculated out of the heavy manufacturing environment of the Midwest. He was highly energetic and ambitious, with eyes on the presidency of the company. Manufacturing efficiency was his mantra, at all cost, and he had most likely never met a customer that wasn't visiting the factory. He was most proud of his inspection pass rate for a line of relatively complex laboratory instruments, which averaged a 99.8% pass rate. Unfortunately, we had very high failures in the field and our warranty expenses were running at twice the industry norm for similar products. Something was amiss.

On further inspection we discovered that yes, 99.8% of the instruments passed the inspection bench, but it took anywhere from two to three weeks for each instrument to pass inspection. They had fallen into a nether world of tinkering and hidden rework that masked serious issues in the design and manufacturing process. Eventually, the instability of the instruments would show up in the laboratories of our customers. A key truism of the Total Quality Management movement is *you can't inspect quality into a product* and this was definitely evident here.

When this issue was addressed in the quality meeting a major political battle erupted. Rather than expend energy on addressing the underlying issues, the leader of our manufacturing unit spent his energy twisting a fundamental quality issue into a series of personal attacks towards the marketing team that had revealed a serious customer issue. Not very rational, yet this executive's political capital was sufficient to bury the issue (along with several marketers' careers within the company) and turn the quality team meetings into a charade.

I witnessed similar issue in the mid-nineties as the executive in charge of global service for a company that manufactured custom machinery for manufacturing pharmaceutical products. Customer-driven design specifications were critical in both the operation and validation of these complex machines. If the machines didn't operate to the specification, they couldn't pass internal validation. Worse, this also placed the customers' manufacturing at risked of being non-compliant with FDA regulations.

Our field service team consistently found itself rebuilding the machines in the field because the systems were not meeting the process qualifications and tests conducted by our customers. With profit and loss (P&L) responsibility for the business unit, this was rapidly eroding our team's financial performance. In addition, it was destroying our credibility in front of our customers. The president of the sales team approached me to build a case against the manufacturing unit, that somehow they were not building the systems properly and were costing the business additional sales. Upon further investigation with my field service personnel, we were able to document the fact that manufacturing was building the equipment exactly to the specifications they were given. Manufacturing was doing its job and doing it well. In addition, our service personnel were expert at installation and operational qualifications, and we had created voluminous testing documents to ensure our procedures complied with the customers' validation requirements. So where did the problem lie?

Our team dove into the entire specification process and documented process maps of what was occurring in each sale. We quickly discovered and were able to prove that the fault was with the sales team. They were very aggressive and quick to secure a purchase order, but felt their job was done at that point. They were off to the next prospect in order to close another sale. When the installation and start-up tests with the customer failed, they blamed service for not knowing how to properly do their jobs, or blamed manufacturing. Unfortunately, the salespeople were not taking the time to fully understand the customers' manufacturing criteria and were selling them the wrong configurations of the machines, which, by definition, were incapable of doing the job designated by the customers. When we presented these process maps in a joint meeting of engineering, sales, service, and manufacturing, the president of the sales unit blew a gasket! Once again, the messengers of this critical-to-quality information were chastised and personally attacked. Rationality flew out the window in favor of the emotionally-driven blame game.

The point I'm trying to make is any system of measuring performance can be gamed. By thoroughly understanding and documenting critical-to-quality processes you can begin to measure by exception to performance. But you must understand exactly what is happening at each touchpoint of the process before you can measure any significant variation to the process. And keep in mind, human beings are emotionally-driven creatures. By assuming people may not act rationally in the best interests of the customer and the business (often through no fault of their own...they're simply unconscious of this phenomena) we can begin to create standard operating procedures that take human fallibility into account.

Another key aspect to keep in mind is you're going to get the behavior you pay for. The head of manufacturing I discussed had a bonus tied to pass rate, not warranty expenses. This enabled him to game the system in his favor while shortchanging the customers and the overall business. In the other example, the president of the sales group and his salespeople were paid on sales, not successful system start-ups and validations, so they ran as fast as they could to land the next sale without concern for the lasting impact on the customer or the company. By thinking from the perspective of how what we do affects our customers we can begin to align compensation models to the desired behavior that most benefits our customers, and in turn, our company.

These are great examples of how functionality (or disfunctionality) is affected by organizational structure. Both of these organizations were relatively large hierarchies. There were layers of management, support, and field sales/service between the customer and the leaders that demonstrated such short sighted behavior. The leaders were comfortably insulated from the results of their leadership. A conduit structure places the leadership in close proximity to customer-centric, value creating (or destroying) processes that directly impact the customer. It places leaders on the front line, where they belong. To paraphrase General George Patton, leading people is like leading a rope, you cannot push it from behind, you have to get out in front and pull it.

~ Key Concepts

- How we structure a business is a reflection of how we perceive function, and once established, how we function is highly influenced by our organizational structure.
- Hierarchies lead to silos and intransigent bureaucracies that isolate leadership from customers.
- New ways of thinking and performing require new organizational structures.
- You cannot manage something that you cannot measure, but you must know how what you are measuring is critical to your customers' objectives.
- You will inevitably get the behavior you're paying for. Align compensation as closely as possible to positive customer outcomes and value creation from their perspectives.

~ Exercise

Create a process map following an order throughout your entire fulfillment process. Where do human-driven variables come into play? How can they affect your customers? How can your processes be brought into alignment with customer value creation?

Coda

"Success is the ability to go from one failure to another with no loss of enthusiasm." Winston Churchill

When I set out to write this book I did so with two things in mind. First, I felt there was a glaring need in the marketplace for a book that explained, step-by-step, how leading and managing from a mindful, highly conscious perspective can fully engage the cumulative, creative capabilities of human beings in an organization, driving profound productivity and performance. There seemed to be plenty of books that said, "think this way and become a millionaire" or "be this way and you'll automatically attract success and wealth", but none of these authors seemed ready to offer historically validated steps and methods necessary to fulfill the promise of their philosophies.

Second, I felt compelled to sort out and share the business lessons I paid so dearly for over the years. I took some hard knocks along the way until I figured out I simply didn't belong in the corporate cultures I found myself in. I had something these executives desperately wanted; my strategic planning skills combined with my ability to rapidly ignite positive change that drove breakthrough performance. What they didn't anticipate was the very essence of what enabled me to deliver such unprecedented organizational success was incongruent with their own intention and perspective on what it meant to be a leader. They wanted change, accountability, and increased performance. Unfortunately, in many instances, they weren't prepared to embrace the fact that this needed to come from themselves as well as their employees.

As you can see, there are no secrets to leading a successful business. Neither are there any quick fixes or vapid mantras that will magically turn things around with the slightest of effort. While nuanced and multi-layered, in the end, leading a thriving business comes down to one common denominator - you. How you choose to be is as important, if not more important, as what you choose to do.

Preparing and building for success is similar to weaving a tapestry. Skipping one thread here or there will introduce a flaw, but it may very well go unnoticed. But skipping many threads as a short cut to success will cause the entire endeavor to eventually unravel. Leadership is intertwined with strategy, culture, presence, and execution. When authentic leadership is embraced, when we hold ourselves accountable and acknowledge the responsibilities that come with that mantle. When this emerges, pulling upon a single thread will move the entire tapestry as one...it will not unravel within our hands.

Throughout this book, we spoke at length and in detail about the strategic planning process and the impact of a creative culture. Perhaps you noticed that the leadership lessons were intrinsically woven into these processes. This wasn't contrived, it is where these lessons emerged for me throughout my career. It was through action and engagement, from a mind-set of simply trying to be a decent and respectful human being, that I emerged as a leader. It was not until later in life that I was able to look back with a somewhat enlightened perspective and realize the essence of what was happening just beneath the surface. These quiet forces are eternal; they are constantly present if we only choose to see them.

Most of us can probably agree, corporate business models are broken and misaligned with human beings and our environment. We, as entrepreneurs, can affect change, but as Mahatma Gandhi advised, "Be the change you want to see in the world." This is where we must start, with our selves. I know the approaches we have explored in this book work. I've lived them firsthand. I sincerely believe the way to impart a shift in our corporate landscape is to simply out-compete the old paradigm. The methodologies and mind-sets discussed in this book offer us a way forward; a way to out-prosper the old guard and secure their attention and help them recognize their need for change. As traditional companies lose market share and profits to enlightened companies they will sit up and take notice. In this way, we can be the change our world desperately needs.

Illustrations

The Transformational Entrepreneur

Index

D

Index

Index

Index